Presented To
Cedar Mill Community Library

In memory of
Stanley Hartman

KEEP IT REAL

KEEP IT REAL

Everything
You Need to Know
About Researching
and Writing
Creative Nonfiction

Edited by Lee Gutkind
and Hattie Fletcher

W. W. Norton & Company
New York   London

For information about special discounts for bulk purchases, please contact
    W. W. Norton Special Sales at specialsales@wwnorton.com or 800-233-4830

Manufacturing by Courier Westford
Book design by Anna Oler

Library of Congress Cataloging-in-Publication Data

Keep it real : everything you need to know about researching and writing creative nonfiction / edited by Lee Gutkind and Hattie Fletcher. — 1st ed.
    p. cm.
    ISBN 978-0-393-06561-9 (hardcover)
    1. Reportage literature—Authorship. 2. Journalism—Authorship. 3. Creative
writing. I. Gutkind, Lee. II. Buck, Hattie Fletcher.
    PN3377.5.R45K44 2008
    808'.02—dc22

                                        2007042777

W. W. Norton & Company, Inc.
500 Fifth Avenue, New York, N.Y. 10110
www.wwnorton.com

W. W. Norton & Company Ltd.
Castle House, 75/76 Wells Street, London W1T 3QT

1 2 3 4 5 6 7 8 9 0

Contents

The ABCs of Creative Nonfiction

Contributing Writers

"The ABCs of Creative Nonfiction" was a group effort, and much of the writing in it evolved significantly over the course of compiling *Keep It Real*. Some of the entries include the work of more than one writer; most of the entries have been reworked by the editors to maintain a consistent tone and eliminate repetitions. For this reason, individual pieces are not credited to specific writers. The writers who contributed work are:

Robert S. Boynton
Kristen Cosby
Taha Ebrahimi
Hattie Fletcher
Lee Gutkind
Meredith Hall
Donna Hogarty
Kristen Iversen
Lori Jakiela
Barbara Lounsberry

Brenda Miller
Dinty W. Moore
Paul Morris
Dennis Palumbo
Lori Pfeiffer
Mimi Schwartz
Bryant Simon
Kathleen Tarr
Sarah Z. Wexler
Susan Yohe

Private and Public: The Range and Scope of Creative Nonfiction

Lee Gutkind

This may come as a surprise, since I am often referred to as "the godfather behind creative nonfiction" (so anointed by *Vanity Fair* magazine), but I don't know who actually coined the term "creative nonfiction." As far as I know, nobody knows exactly. I have been using it since the 1970s, although if we were to pinpoint a time when the term became "official," it would be 1983, at a meeting convened by the National Endowment for the Arts to deal with the question of what to call the genre as a category for the NEA's creative writing fellowships. Initially the fellowships bestowed grant money (seventy-five hundred dollars at the time; twenty thousand dollars today) only to poets and fiction writers, although the NEA had long recognized the "art" of nonfiction and been trying to find a way to describe the category so writers would understand what kind of work to submit for consideration.

"Essay" is the term used to describe this "artful" nonfiction, but it didn't really capture the essence of the genre for the NEA or lots of other folks experimenting in the field. Technically, scholars, critics, and academics of all sorts, as well as newspaper op-ed reporters, were writing "essays," although that was not the kind of work the NEA had in mind. "Journalism" didn't fit the category either, although the anchoring element of the best creative nonfiction requires an aspect of reportage. For a while the NEA experimented with "belles-lettres," a misunderstood term that favors style over substance and did not capture the personal essence and foundation of the literature it was seeking. Eventually one of the NEA members in the meeting that day pointed out that a rebel in his English department was campaigning for the term "creative nonfiction." I was that rebel.

Although it sounds a bit affected and presumptuous, "creative nonfiction" precisely describes what the form is all about. The word "creative" refers simply to the use of literary craft in presenting nonfiction—that is, factually accurate prose about real people and events—in a compelling, vivid manner. To put it another way, creative nonfiction writers do not make things up; they make ideas and information that already exist more interesting and often more accessible.

This general meaning of the term is basically acknowledged and accepted in the literary world; poets, fiction writers, and the creative writing community in general understand and accept the elements of creative nonfiction, although their individual interpretation of the genre's boundaries may differ. The essential point to acknowledge here is that there are lines, real demarcation points among fiction, which is or can be mostly imagination; traditional nonfiction (journalism and scholarship), which is mostly information; and creative nonfiction, which presents or treats information using the tools of the fiction writer while maintaining allegiance to fact.

There is, it is true, controversy over the legitimacy of creative nonfiction, both as a term and as a genre; it flares up regularly, perhaps even annually, every time a book like James

Frey's *A Million Little Pieces*, which purported to be a memoir but contains fictionalized events, is unmasked. Such scandals seem to inspire frenzies among literary and cultural critics, an excuse for predictable (but nevertheless often satisfying) expressions of schadenfreude and sanctimonious pronouncements about Truth in Art.

Ultimately, this controversy over the form or the word is not only rather silly but moot; the genre itself, the practice of writing nonfiction in a dramatic and imaginative way, has been an anchoring element of the literary world for many years. George Orwell's *Down and Out in Paris and London*, James Baldwin's *Notes of a Native Son*, Ernest Hemingway's *Death in the Afternoon*, and Tom Wolfe's *The Right Stuff* are classic creative nonfiction efforts, books that communicate information (reportage) in a scenic, dramatic fashion.

These four books represent the full spectrum of creative nonfiction: Baldwin's work is memoir and therefore more personal or inward, dealing with the dynamics of his relationship with his father and the burden of race in America; Wolfe's work is more journalistic or outward, capturing the lives of the early astronauts. *Death in the Afternoon* and *Down and Out in Paris and London* fall somewhere in between—personal, like memoir, but filled with information about bullfighting and poverty respectively. I often refer to this combination as the parallel narratives of creative nonfiction; there is almost always a "public" and a "private" story.

At one point in history this kind of writing gained popularity as the New Journalism, in large part because of Wolfe, who published a book of that title in 1973. In it, he declared that the New Journalism "would wipe out the novel as literature's main event." Gay Talese, in the introduction to *Fame and Obscurity*, his landmark collection of profiles of public figures including Frank Sinatra, Joe DiMaggio, and Peter O'Toole, describes the New Journalism thus: "Though often reading like fiction, [it] is not fiction. It is, or should be, as reliable as the most reliable reportage, although it seeks a larger truth than is possible through the mere compilation of verifiable facts, the use of direct quotations, and adherence to the rigid organizational style of the older form."

This is perhaps creative nonfiction's greatest asset: It offers flexibility and freedom while adhering to the basic tenets of reportage. In creative nonfiction, writers can be poetic and journalistic simultaneously. Creative nonfiction writers are encouraged to utilize literary and even cinematic techniques, from scene to dialogue to description to point of view, to write about themselves and others, capturing real people and real life in ways that can and have changed the world. What is most important and enjoyable about creative nonfiction is that it not only allows but also encourages the writer to become a part of the story or essay being written. The personal involvement creates a special magic that alleviates the suffering and anxiety of the writing experience; it provides many outlets for satisfaction and self-discovery, flexibility and freedom.

The Creative Nonfiction Police

Many writers have come to creative nonfiction seeking more freedom than is usually allowed by the narrow confines of traditional journalism, which not only demands a certain form, usually measured in inches, but sometimes requires that writers suppress their hard-earned expertise in a topic to maintain an appropriate detachment, or "objectivity." Yet journalists hardly constitute the majority of creative nonfiction writers. One of the major reasons for the sudden and growing popularity of the genre is that poets and fiction writers have also entered into it with great enthusiasm, experimenting with and pushing the parameters of the form. The long list of respected poets and novelists who have written landmark books and essays in creative nonfiction includes Norman Mailer, Diane Ackerman, William Styron, and W. S. Merwin, as a barest beginning. Without endorsement and experimentation by writers whose reputation was made in other genres, creative nonfiction could not have grown at the astounding rate it has. Since the early 1990s there has been an explosion of creative nonfiction. Many of our best magazines—the *New Yorker, Harper's, Vanity Fair, Esquire*—publish more creative nonfiction than fiction and poetry combined. Every year more universities in the United States and throughout the world offer Master of Fine Arts degrees in creative nonfiction.

All this flexibility—writers crossing genres, applying tools from poetry and fiction to true stories, the connection between the personal and the public—has made some people, writers of creative nonfiction included, uncomfortable and confused. I often give talks to groups of students and other aspiring writers. Invariably, people in the audience ask questions about what writers can or can't do, stylistically and in content, while writing creative nonfiction. The freedom provided by the expanded boundaries is perplexing. The questioners are unrelenting: "How can you be certain that the dialogue you are remembering and re-creating from an incident that occurred months ago is accurate?"; "How can you look through the eyes of your characters if you are not inside their heads?"

I always answer as best I can. I try to explain that such questions have a lot to do with a writer's ethical and moral boundaries and, most important, how hard writers are willing to work to achieve accuracy and believability in their narratives. Making up a story or elaborating extemporaneously on a situation that did, in fact, occur can be interesting but unnecessary. Truth is often more compelling to contemplate than fiction. But the questions and the confusion about what a writer can or cannot do often persist—for too long.

Once, at a college in Texas, I finally threw up my hands in frustration and said, "Listen, I can't answer all these questions with rules and regulations. I am not," I announced, pausing rather theatrically, "the creative nonfiction police!"

There was a woman in the audience—someone I had noticed earlier during my reading; she was in the front row: hard to miss—older than most of the undergraduates, blond, attractive, in her late thirties maybe. She had the alert yet composed look of a nurse, a person only semirelaxed, always ready to act or react. She had taken off her shoes and propped her feet on the stage. I remember how her toes wiggled as she laughed at the essay I had been reading.

When I made my dramatic announcement, this woman suddenly jumped to her feet, whipped out a badge, and pointed in my direction. "Well, I am," she announced. "Someone has to be. And you are under arrest."

Then she scooped up her shoes and stormed barefooted from the room. The Q and A ended soon after, and I rushed into the hallway to find the woman with the badge. I had many questions, beginning with "Who the hell are you? Why do you have a badge? And how did you know what I was going to say when I didn't have any idea?" I had never used the term "creative nonfiction police" before that moment. But she was gone.

My host said the woman was a stranger. We asked around, but no one knew her. She was a mystery to everyone, especially me, and remains so to this day.

The Five Rs

The bigger mystery, however, then and now, is the debate that triggered my symbolic arrest, the set of parameters that govern or define creative nonfiction and the questions writers must consider while laboring in or struggling with what some call the literature of reality.

I meant what I said to that audience—I am not the creative nonfiction police—but working on the journal *Creative Nonfiction* means that my staff and I have had to make many decisions about where its parameters lie. And so, although we won't lay down the law, we will define some of the essential elements of creative nonfiction.

Basic public education once covered the three Rs: reading, 'riting, and 'rithmetic. I find it's helpful to think of the basic tenets of creative nonfiction in a similar manner, with the addition of two more Rs.

The first R is the real-life aspect of the writing experience. As a writing teacher I design assignments that have an immersion aspect. I force my students out into their communities for an hour, a day, or even a week so that they see and understand that the foundation of good writing is personal experience. I've sent my students to police stations, bagel shops, golf courses; together my classes have gone on excursions and participated in public service projects, all in an attempt to experience, and to re-create from experience, real life.

Which is not to say that all creative nonfiction has to involve the writer's immersion into the experiences of others. Some writers (and students) may utilize their own personal experiences. In one introductory course I taught, a young man working his way through school as a salesperson wrote about selling shoes, while another student, who served as a volunteer in a hospice, captured a dramatic moment of death, grief, and family relief.

Not only were these essays, and many others my students have written over the years, based on real life, but they also contained personal messages from writer to reader, which gave them extra meaning. "An essay is when I write what I think about something," students will often say to me. Which is true, to a certain extent, and also the source of the meaning of the second R, reflection. In creative nonfiction, unlike in traditional journalism, a writer's feelings and responses about a subject are permitted and encouraged. But essays can't just be personal opinion; writers have to reach out to readers in a number of different and compelling ways.

This reaching out is essential if a writer hopes to find an audience. *Creative Nonfiction* receives approximately three hundred unsolicited essays a month. The vast majority of these submissions are rejected, and one common reason is an overwhelming egocentrism. In other words, writers write too much about themselves and what they think without seeking a universal focus so that readers are properly and firmly engaged. Essays that are so personal that they omit the reader are essays that will never see the light of print. The overall objective of a writer should be to make the reader tune in, not out.

Another main reason *Creative Nonfiction* and many other journals and magazines reject essays is a lack of attention to another essential element of the creative nonfiction genre, which is to gather and present information, to teach readers about a person, place, idea, or situation, combining the creativity of the artistic experience with the essential third R in the formula, research or reportage. Even the most personal essay is usually full of substantive detail about a subject that affects or concerns the writer.

Personal experience, research, and spontaneous intellectual discourse—an airing and exploration of ideas—are equally vital elements in creative nonfiction. Annie Dillard, another prominent creative nonfiction writer, takes great pains to achieve this balance in her work. In her first book, *Pilgrim at Tinker Creek*, which won a Pulitzer Prize, and in her other books and essays, Dillard bombards her readers with factual information—minutely detailed descriptions of insects, botany and biology, history and anthropology—blended with her own feelings about life.

One of my favorite Dillard essays, "Schedules," focuses on the importance of writers working on a regular schedule rather than only intermittently. In this essay she discusses, among many other subjects, Hasidism, chess, baseball, warblers, pine trees, June bugs, writers' studios, and potted plants, as well as her own schedule and writing habits and those of Wallace Stevens and Jack London.

What I am saying is that the genre of creative nonfiction is open to anyone with a curious mind and a sense of self. The research phase actually launches and anchors the creative effort. Whether it is a book or essay I am planning, I always begin my quest in the library (or, increasingly, online), for three reasons. First, I need to familiarize myself with the subject. If I don't know much about it, I want to make myself knowledgeable enough to ask intelligent questions when I begin interviewing people. If I can't display at least a minimal understanding of the subject about which I want to write, I will lose the confidence and support of the people who can provide me access to the experience.

Second, I want to assess my competition. What other essays, books, and articles have been written about this subject? Who are the experts, the pioneers, the most controversial figures? I want to find a new angle, not write a story similar to one that has already been written. Finally, how can I reflect on and evaluate a person, subject, or place unless I know all the contrasting points of view? Reflection may permit a certain amount of speculation but only when based on a solid foundation of knowledge.

This brings me to the fourth R, reading. Writers must read not only research material unearthed in the library but also the work of the masters of their profession. I have heard some very fine writers claim that they don't read too much anymore or that they don't read for long periods, especially during the time they are laboring on a lengthy writing project. But almost all writers have read the best writers in their field and are able to converse in great detail about their stylistic approaches and the intellectual content of their work, much as any good visual artist is able to discuss the work of Picasso, van Gogh, Michelangelo, and Warhol.

Finally, there's the fifth R, the 'riting, the most artistic and romantic aspect of the whole experience. The first four Rs relate to the nonfiction part of creative nonfiction; this last R is where writers get to create. Writing often happens in two phases: Usually there is an inspirational explosion at the beginning, a time when writers allow instinct and feeling to guide their fingers as they create paragraphs, pages, and even entire chapters or complete essays. This is what art of any form is all about: the passion of the moment and the magic of the muse. I am not saying it always happens; it doesn't. Writing is a difficult labor in which a daily grind or struggle (ideally with a regular schedule, as Annie Dillard concludes) is necessary. But this first part of the experience—for most writers, most of the time—is rather loose and spontaneous and, therefore, more creative and fun. The second part of the writing experience, the craft part, which comes into play after your basic essay is written, is equally important and a hundred times more difficult.

The Building Blocks of Creative Nonfiction: Scene, Dialogue, Intimate Detail, and Other Essentials

The craft part means the construction of the essay (or chapter or even book): how the research, reflection, and real-life experience are arranged to make a story meaningful and important to readers.

The primary way this is accomplished in creative nonfiction is through the use of scene. In fact, one of the most obvious distinguishing factors between traditional journalism and creative nonfiction—or simply between ordinary prose and good, evocative writing—is the use of vignettes, episodes, and other slices of reality. The uninspired writer will tell the reader about a subject, place, or personality, but the creative nonfiction writer will show that subject, place, or personality in action.

A valuable element of scene is dialogue, people saying things to one another, expressing themselves. Collecting dialogue is one of the reasons writers immerse themselves at a police station, bagel shop, or zoo. It lets them discover what people have to say spontaneously, not just in response to a reporter's questions.

Another technique that helps writers create scene may be described as intimate and specific detail. This is a lesson that writers of all genres need to know: The secret to making prose (or, for that matter, poetry) memorable—and therefore vital and important—is to catalog with specificity the details that are most intimate. By "intimate," I mean ideas and images that readers won't easily imagine, ideas and images you have observed that symbolize a memorable truth about the characters or the situations about which you are writing. "Intimate" means recording and noting details that the reader might not know or even imagine without your particular insight. Sometimes intimate detail can be so specific and special that it becomes unforgettable in the reader's mind.

A very famous "intimate" detail appears in a classic creative nonfiction profile, "Frank Sinatra Has a Cold," written by Gay Talese in 1962 and published in *Esquire*. In this profile, Talese leads readers on a whirlwind cross-country tour, revealing Sinatra and his entourage interacting with one another and with the rest of the world and demonstrating how Sinatra's world and the world inhabited by everyone else often collide. The scenes are action-oriented; they contain dialogue and evocative description, including a moment when Talese spotted a gray-haired lady with two hatboxes in the shadows of the Sinatra entourage and put her in the story. She was, it turned out, the guardian of Sinatra's collection of toupees. This tiny detail, Sinatra's wig lady, made such an impression when I first read the essay that even now, years later, anytime I see Sinatra on television or in rerun movies or spot his photo in a magazine, I find myself searching the background for the gray-haired lady with the hatbox.

The gray-haired lady was a detail that readers wouldn't have known about if Talese hadn't shown it to them, and her constant presence there in the shadows, hovering to service or replace Sinatra's toupee, offered important insight into Sinatra's character. And although we can't achieve such symbolism each time we capture an incident, writers who want their words to be remembered beyond the dates on which their stories are published or broadcast will seek to discover the special observations that symbolize the intimacy they have attained with their subjects.

Of course, all these vividly told scenes have to be organized according to some larger plan to make a complete story. We call this plan, or structure, the frame of the story. The frame represents a way of ordering or controlling a writer's narrative so that the elements of his book, article, or essay are presented in an interesting and orderly fashion with an interlaced integrity from beginning to end.

The most basic frame is a simple beginning-to-end chronology, a story that begins at one point and ends at a later point. For a variety of reasons, however, writers often choose not to frame their stories in a strictly chronological sequence. Starting a story in the middle of events can draw readers in and heighten suspense. However the frame is organized, it should help readers identify the main themes, or focus, of the story.

Keep It Real

Finally, harder to define than the elements of craft are all the ethical and moral issues writers of creative nonfiction have to consider. This is actually the way *Keep It Real* started, the reason for its existence. The editors of *Creative Nonfiction* were dismayed by the scandalous controversy over *A Million Little Pieces* and the debacle that followed. Of course, this was not the first time such a brouhaha over truth and accuracy in nonfiction writing had erupted. Some of us remember the debate over the legitimacy of the work of Edmund Morris, a Pulitzer Prize–winning biographer who, while writing the authorized biography of Ronald Reagan, created himself as a fictional character in order to flesh out Reagan's hidden and puzzling personality. To be fair, Morris was not misleading his readers; his act of fictionalizing himself was made clear in the text of *Dutch*. This decision, however, to publish an authorized biography as a fictionalized memoir, created an uproar that was covered in the *New York Times*, on *60 Minutes*, and elsewhere.

Each time a new controversy rages I cringe, for the media tend to indict the genre or the form along with the individual violators of the basic line between fiction and nonfiction. So much of this revolves around individual personal and moral ethical parameters. From Morris's point of view, he was doing his best to reveal the three-dimensional aspects of the historical figure he was attempting to portray. He was upfront with his breach of form; the media responded, as is often the case, in an overly rambunctious manner, turning an interesting literary experiment into an opportunity to pontificate.

To be fair, the examination of the ethical boundaries in Morris's case was thorough and, to a certain extent, valuable in that the inherent problem in creative nonfiction, violating the line between truth and imagination, was delineated and discussed. The controversy over Frey, probably because of Oprah Winfrey's active engagement, was over the top, a fact that motivated us at *Creative Nonfiction* to prepare a special issue,

"A Million Little Choices," to lay out guidelines for the genre, presenting questions, controversies, and conflicts for writers and readers to consider.

As soon as the issue was published, the immediate and overwhelmingly positive response told us that we had addressed a need and satisfied a growing unrest about the dos and don'ts of the form. *Keep It Real* expands upon the original journal issue and includes even more topics.

Keep It Real was a group effort. In order to be thorough and to isolate and explain the aspects of the genre that trigger so many questions and so much concern, we reached out to a network of great writers and editors and knowledgeable experts in the field. These contributors present a range of opinions and ideas about creative nonfiction. We do not mean to suggest that they are a hardbound set of rules, simply that these are issues writers ought to consider when working in this genre.

As much as I would like to take credit as the founder of the form or the term, creative nonfiction is an art form that is defined by all the people who write it. In the end the literature that is created defines itself, and as writers push the boundaries and experiment with imaginative daring, the definition and the guidelines will change. Art, as we know it, is always in flux. That is what makes the process of writing both challenging and eminently and consistently worthwhile.

The ABCs
of Creative
Nonfiction

Acknowledgment of Sources

In April 2004 Bryony Lavery's play *Frozen* debuted on Broadway. It received rave reviews, garnering Tony nominations for the play, its two stars, and the director. Lavery basked in the success—at least until the psychiatrist Dorothy Lewis read the play's script and hired a lawyer.

Lewis said many scenes in the play were based on her memoir, *Guilty by Reason of Insanity: A Psychiatrist Explores the Minds of Killers*, about her life spent working with serial killers. Lewis also noted 12 verbatim quotations, around 675 words in all, taken from a profile written about her by Malcolm Gladwell for the *New Yorker* in 1997. Lewis wanted to sue the playwright, who she thought had stolen details of both her life and her book. Because of the inherent complications of intellectual copyright, however, she eventually dropped the case, and the only place Lavery was judged was in the court of public opinion.

Gladwell, whose prose appears, uncredited, in the play, initially supported Lewis's lawsuit and offered to assign her the copyright to his article. After reading the script of *Frozen*, however, he had a change of heart. He deemed the play "breathtaking" and wrote, in a subsequent article for the *New Yorker*, that "instead of feeling that my words had been taken from me, I felt that they had become part of some grander cause." He found himself sympathizing with the playwright: "Bryony Lavery had seen one of my articles, responded to what she read and used it as she constructed a work of art. And now her reputation was in tatters. Something about that didn't seem right."*

Certainly, many writers, of creative nonfiction and other genres, use newspaper or magazine clippings or traits of someone they know as the genesis of a longer work. Susan Orlean's article for the *New Yorker* and subsequent book *The Orchid Thief* gestated from the seed of an article in the *Naples* (Florida) *Daily News*. So why didn't the *New York Times* write stories suggesting that Orlean's influential work might be plagiarism? The first difference between Orlean and Lavery is one of language: Orlean didn't lift entire passages of someone else's writing; the words were her own. The second, equally important difference is one of facts: Orlean did her own research, spending innumerable hours interviewing the "thief" of her book's title, John Laroche, walking through orchid shows and everglade swamps, and finding facts with her own eyes and ears. Though the idea came from someone else's writing, the final product is a completely different work, one that relies on Orlean's creativity and research—her facts, her interviews, her insights.

Many writers' ideas start with files of newspaper clippings, and it's perfectly fine to let world or local news generate ideas. But the care to avoid plagiarism comes in the following steps,

*In the spirit of fairly acknowledging sources, the anecdote and quotations come from Malcolm Gladwell's wonderfully complex exploration of plagiarism, "Something Borrowed: Should a Charge of Plagiarism Ruin your Life?" published in the *New Yorker*, November 22, 2004.

ensuring that all the language in the writing is your own and citing the sources of quotes, facts, and thematic ideas to give credit to other writers and thinkers the same way you'd want to be acknowledged for your own work.

Today many people are distrustful of what they see and read in the media. Creative nonfiction writers have a complicated obligation to their readers: to entertain like novelists but to educate like journalists. As a result, they have to balance the need for a good story with good facts, and the facts aren't good if they're lifted, without giving credit, from someone else. In *Fast Food Nation*, an indictment of the fast-food industry, Eric Schlosser made his writing nearly bulletproof by including a sixty-seven-page appendix on sources and a bibliography. Whenever Schlosser's reporting wasn't firsthand, he acknowledged what wasn't his own and cited where he had found the information. This not only protected him against potential attacks from fast-food industry lawyers but encouraged the readers' trust and safeguarded his reputation. This is a move all writers can steal, guilt-free.

Backdoor Access

Gay Talese is a master at getting interviews—or making do without them, if need be. Having arrived in Los Angeles in 1965 to interview Frank Sinatra for *Esquire*, Talese was met with the news that the great singer would not be meeting with him as scheduled; not only were there concerns about various topics (like Sinatra's possible friendship with Mafia leaders) that might end up in an article, but Ol' Blue Eyes was also suffering from a head cold and consequently in a foul mood.

Blocked from sitting down with Sinatra, Talese spent a week interviewing people who had interacted with Sinatra in varying capacities over the years. In "Not Interviewing Frank Sinatra," Talese explained, "From most of these people I got something: a tiny nugget of information here, a bit of color there, small pieces for a large mosaic that I hoped would reflect the man who for decades had commanded the spotlight."

The next week Talese tried again to reschedule the interview, but Sinatra still had a cold and refused to meet with him. Talese spent the week interviewing people who had worked for Sinatra, as well as his favorite haberdasher, his son, one of his bodyguards, and the woman who tended his toupees.

And then Frank Sinatra's public relations manager called. "I hear you're all over town seeing Frank's friends, taking Frank's friends to dinner," he said.

Sinatra still didn't want to sit for an interview, but the publicist invited Talese to accompany him to a television taping the next afternoon, a scene that ultimately became a major part of Talese's story "Frank Sinatra Has a Cold," the end product of six weeks of relentless legwork that never did include an interview with the singer.

It didn't matter, though. Talese writes in the introduction to *Fame and Obscurity*: "I gained more by watching him, overhearing him, and observing the reactions of those around him than if I had actually been able to sit down and talk to him."

Talese credits his success, both then and now, to persistence. "It's about selling yourself," he explains. "It's all about hanging around and meeting people."

Lee Gutkind, the editor and founder of *Creative Nonfiction*, has had several similar backdoor access experiences. "Persistence is the key," he says. "If it doesn't look like you're going to get your access by going straight to the boss, don't waste your time. Go around him, and you'll get there in the end."

Gutkind used the backdoor to gain access to the organ transplant world for his book *Many Sleepless Nights: The World of Organ Transplantation* because he knew that approaching the surgeons in the field right off the bat would be difficult. Surgeons, after all, are very busy people. So Gutkind started attending patient support meetings and befriended a few patients. Unlike the surgeons, the patients and their families had all the time in the world. The patients were always in bed, while the family members were always sitting around, smoking, drinking coffee, and waiting for the doctor.

Gutkind spent an average of four hours a day, five days a

week with his subjects, sitting in their hospital rooms and accompanying them to doctor appointments. "Over nine or ten months, the doctors were seeing me all the time because I was with the patients. At that point it was just natural for them to ask me what I was doing, and that became my entry point to their part of the transplant world.

"You simply need to be willing to take the time," Gutkind says. "And it's frustrating and costly. You're investing this time, and it usually doesn't seem like you're getting anything back. You could be immersed in your subject for an entire year and not even have a first chapter."

This is one reason that readers turn to books; they don't have time to experience everything for themselves. Instead of spending a year with the subject, readers get the experience in the time it takes to read just a chapter. It is the writer's job to gain that access for the reader, and the process can be a painstaking, often creative, sometimes frustrating and time-consuming part of writing a story. Gaining access requires an ability to change strategy and be flexible but mostly to like hanging out with more than just the central stars.

Checkbook Journalism

In November 1970 *Esquire* published one of its most memorable covers ever. Illustrating "The Confessions of Lt. Calley," the first of three articles about the man who led his platoon in the murder of hundreds of Vietnamese civilians in My Lai, it consisted of a photograph of Calley, in full uniform and grinning broadly, surrounded by four adorable Asian children.

Perhaps Calley was smiling because *Esquire* had paid $20,000 (the equivalent of more than $100,000 today) for his exclusive cooperation with the veteran journalist John Sack, who received $10,000 for writing the articles. And this wasn't the only instance of *Esquire*'s paying the subject of a story; in 1963 the magazine had promised Muhammad Ali (then Cassius Clay) $150 ($1,000 in today's dollars) to cooperate with a young journalist named Tom Wolfe for "The Marvelous Mouth," which it published in its October issue.

That these two clear instances of checkbook journalism were published during *Esquire*'s golden era, when it was edited by the legendary Harold Hayes, makes one wonder: Can journalistic greatness coexist with a practice associated with sleazy celebrity magazines and tabloid television?

In the wake of the James Frey, Stephen Glass, and Jayson

Blair scandals, contemporary journalists and educators have become obsessed with the profession's ethics. And there is no principle about which they are more adamant than the one prohibiting any kind of monetary exchange between a writer and the subject of his story. In today's ethical climate, a journalist who questions any aspect of this principle risks forfeiting his journalistic integrity.

The arguments against checkbook journalism are obvious. The promise of cash for information creates an incentive to tell a journalist what he wants to hear, regardless of whether it is the truth. There is always the possibility that subjects will lie and that journalists will make mistakes, but the less likely it is that they have a financial relationship, the more likely it is that something approximating the truth will find its way into the next day's paper.

But does the prohibition hold in every instance? It would obviously be a bad idea for a daily reporter to go around handing twenty-dollar bills out to everyone he interviews. But what about the magazine or book writer who spends months, perhaps years, trailing his subjects? Do the reporter's ethical constraints apply when he is interviewing a character dozens of times, depriving him or her of every shred of privacy, or when his project depends completely on his subject's continuous and willing participation? Does such a journalist—especially one working for highly remunerative magazines or whose books become best sellers and perhaps even movies—really owe his subjects *nothing*? Is the difference between rules guiding the daily reporter and the magazine writer one of degree or of kind?

In fact, one might argue that some kind of exchange is inherent in every immersion-based reporting project, that there are no such things as selfless subjects or reporters. One character cooperates in order to publicize his message; another wants to be famous and possibly even rich; some desire revenge. And among the reasons the professional journalist writes, of course, is the pay.

The fear of being branded with a scarlet *C* keeps all but the most intrepid journalists from ever thinking about the gray territory that lies between outright money for information checkbook journalism and that in which the writer is self-conscious about his debt to his subjects. The examples of those few who have are suggestive.

In the epilogue to *There Are No Children Here*, Alex Kotlowitz explains that the family he writes about agreed to cooperate with him without any promise of remuneration. After Kotlowitz had finished the book, however, he decided to use some of its proceeds to set up an educational trust fund for the two central characters, a final act of compassion for two boys with whom he formed all sorts of connections while reporting their story. "I know there are some people who will say that I became too involved with the family, that I broke my pact as a journalist to remain detached and objective," he writes.

Jon Krakauer, the author of best sellers like *Into Thin Air* and *Into the Wild*, objects in principle to paying subjects for information. However, he adds that there are some occasions when they "deserve to be compensated for their contributions." For instance, while reporting *Under the Banner of Heaven*, Krakauer paid twenty thousand dollars for the rights to a woman's memoir, even though she had already provided him all the valuable information it contained. He recognized that he had benefited from the exchange and that there might be a way to help her without undermining the integrity of his project. "She was dirt poor and struggling to overcome some serious problems, and I wanted to compensate her for helping me," he explains.

The question of what, whether, or when a long-form journalist owes a source is never going to be straightforward. It is a discussion that takes place at the extremes of journalism, where the extraordinary duration and depth of reporting put the writer-subject relationship in a different light. And for every Alex Kotlowitz and Jon Krakauer, there is a Joe McGinnis, whose contractual relationship with Jeffrey MacDonald (the author agreed to share the proceeds of his book, *Fatal Vision*, and went so far as to join the defense team during the trial) blew up in his face after McGinnis had begun to think MacDonald might be guilty of murder after all.

The point is not that journalists should routinely compensate their sources; in the vast majority of cases, they shouldn't. Rather, it is that we should be suspicious of the knee-jerk way in which journalists invoke the no money for information rule. Isn't it possible that it is simultaneously true and a way of banishing awkward questions of money and exchange from our moral calculations? In the murky intimacy that comes with immersion reporting, reporters sometimes literally owe their subjects *everything*. Perhaps this is why they try to avoid the topic entirely.

Composite Characters[*]

For some writers, a composite character—that is, the melding of two or more real people into one—crosses the line into fiction. Those coming from a journalist tradition in particular find the blurring of characters for whatever reason a violation of the factual base of nonfiction.

For others, however, composite figures make ethical and practical sense. If you are writing about the nonfamous, particularly friends and family who did not ask to be in your story, they expect their confidences to remain confidential. Violating their trust might destroy your relationship with them. Yet you have a story to write, about what you observe and struggle with in the world and about the real people who struggle with you. What to do? Some avoid telling such stories as nonfiction. Others wait until the people involved have died. Still others publish somewhere that those involved won't read . . . they hope. Or they call it fiction and keep their fingers crossed.

Or they opt to write a composite character, particularly if

---

[*]A different version of "Composite Characters" appears in *Writing True: The Art and Craft of Creative Nonfiction*, by Mimi Schwartz and Sondra Perl, published by Houghton Mifflin, 2006.

several people exhibit similar traits. If three friends are getting divorces, for example, and the conversations seem the same, many writers find using a composite character to be more ethical than singling out one soon-to-be ex-friend. The key is to let readers know what you are doing and why. Sometimes a single footnote is enough to maintain the contract between writer and reader, something like "I've changed names and identities to protect the privacy of friends and family, but all else is true as I experienced it."

Some writers give fuller explanations for the use of composites. During the process of writing *36 Views of Mount Fuji*, a memoir about teaching English in Japan, Cathy N. Davidson had writer's block because she feared that "a personal account might be embarrassing to the individual Japanese who inspired it." In the acknowledgments to the book, she explains, "Composite characters . . . allow[ed] me to report actual events but to blur details in order to preserve the anonymity of the people involved." As it turned out, the book was a best seller, and there were no outcries about her memoir's being fiction; clearly, her decision did not hurt the book's reception. Reader outrage, it seems, arises when privacy is not the reason for composites, when readers think there's a more opportunistic motive at work, like trying to make a more dramatic story at truth's expense.

But even when noble reasons are at work, readers can feel manipulated if they find that a character they thought was real turns out to be a composite. That happened when Nobel laureate Rigoberta Menchú wrote about the death of her brother Nicolas in her memoir about Guatemala. When reporters later discovered that Nicolas was alive, Menchú's explanation was that he was a composite figure for all those young men, including another brother, who were murdered or starved to death. For many, the book's credibility was lost; the justification came too late. Had she, like Davidson, put it in the book, perhaps most readers would have thought that the writer-reader pact for "writing true" had been preserved.

Compression

Imagine a writer working on a complicated profile for a magazine, a story about a man with radical, unsettling ideas. If his theories prove to be correct, this man could dramatically change the entire field of psychoanalysis. The writer speaks with him dozens of times, usually using her tape recorder and always taking copious notes. She is determined to understand not only whether his ideas have merit but also if the man himself is trustworthy.

When she pulls together her research and sits down to write, the writer decides to combine parts from many of the interviews she's conducted into one, presenting them as a single, extended conversation that occurred at her first meeting with the subject. This technique, known as compression, allows writers to manage chronology and control the pace of their narratives.

Unfortunately, when the article appears, the man in the profile doesn't like what he reads. In fact, he sues both the writer and the magazine for libel. And much of what he finds objectionable is in the writer's depiction of that first meeting (which wasn't actually one meeting at all).

As you have probably realized, this is a true story. The writer in question, Janet Malcolm, was sued for a hefty sum—$7.5 million, according to the *New York Times*—by Jeffrey Masson, a Sanskrit scholar and psychoanalyst who was also, for a brief time, the curator of the Freud Archives. Malcolm's initial meeting with Masson occurred at the Chez Panisse restaurant in Berkeley, California. In the first installment of her subsequent two-part article for the *New Yorker*, Malcolm used the restaurant as her primary setting for the entire piece, including conversations that did not actually take place there. In a long monologue by Masson that continued for several pages, Malcolm allowed him to reveal his foibles: He seemed at once rash, narcissistic, and voluble.

Masson objected to Malcolm's depiction of him, initially alleging that she had falsified quotes. In fact, Malcolm was generally able to substantiate, with either tape recordings or notes, that she was quoting Masson accurately, although she could not corroborate several of Masson's most damning statements, made during an interview conducted in the kitchen of her New York apartment, not at Chez Panisse, because her tape recorder had been on the blink, her notebook later lost.

The litigation that ensued lasted for ten years and involved two separate trials (the first trial resulted in a hung jury). As the case continued, Masson's attorneys changed tack and went after Malcolm on five particular quotations that she could not substantiate. Although she was not sued for her use of compression per se, Malcolm did acknowledge that she had combined a large number of interviews into one, and Masson's attorneys attempted to use this admission to undermine her credibility. As a result, when compression was brought up while she was on the stand during the second trial, Malcolm was forced to defend the technique. She testified that Masson's pages-long monologue at Chez Panisse was necessary, explaining that his "speaking style is an essential part of his character." The jury in the second trial found in her favor, and Janet Malcolm was finally cleared. But her experience shows that although compression may often be a sound choice artistically, it is also rife with danger.

Other celebrated writers have come under fire for using this technique. Take the case of Vivian Gornick. In the summer of 2003, during Goucher College's low-residency M.F.A. program, Gornick admitted that her memoir *Fierce Attachments* includes a fictitious walk with her mother, an amalgam of many similar walks. (In the aftermath of the ensuing debate, Gornick reframed the controversy by describing her use of the scene as an example of compression.) Gornick's case is, in many respects, quite different from Malcolm's. Memoir presents its own challenges and, to some extent, demands its own set of rules. In the absence of transcripts from interviews, memoirists must re-create scenes and conversations to the best of their abilities. But even when they have transcripts, writers can't just cut and paste from them into stories; literary journalists such as Malcolm often edit out the repetitions, unfinished sentences, and digressions that mar ordinary speech, using a form of compression to present a subject as thoughtful and coherent.

Ironically, Malcolm testified that this concern had motivated her treatment of Masson, stating, "I needed to present [his monologue] in a logical, rational order so he would sound like a logical, rational person." Malcolm's defense goes straight to the heart of the ethical problems raised by this technique. Obviously, all writers omit "ums" and carefully use punctuation to clarify speakers' meanings. But what should a writer do when an exact adherence to chronology will leave the reader bewildered or when a literal rendering will fail to reveal the hidden meaning behind the bare facts? Where does one draw the line? And had Janet Malcolm crossed it? Martin Garbus, a libel lawyer in New York, praised the verdict in an interview with the *New York Times* but added these cautionary words: "What is common is taking large quotes, squishing them and moving them around. What is not common is being as loose as she was. Journalists now know that if you do this, you do it at some risk."

Defamation and Libel

Here are two important tenets of libel law every writer should know: (1) If what you say is true, it cannot be libel, and (2) generally speaking, you can't libel a dead person.

Libel is defined as a false and defamatory statement, in writing, concerning a person, that has been published to a third party. In other words, if John sends a letter about Amy to Amy, that isn't libel. But if John sends a letter about Amy to another person or publishes the letter in a newspaper or other public forum, his words may be libelous, depending on what he's saying about Amy.

"Defamatory," in legal terms, means tending to harm the reputation of the person who is the subject of the statement. We're talking about a statement that is more than just embarrassing or annoying; to be libelous, it must be the kind of statement that would deter other people from associating with that person.

Libel law differs from state to state, but every state's law must conform to the First Amendment prohibition against "abridging the freedom of speech or of the press." To be specific, the First Amendment protects truthful statements. (Publishing truthful statements can sometimes amount to invasion of privacy, but that's a different issue.) Therefore, regardless of variations in libel law, every state's law will provide that only false statements can be libelous.

In general, libel law requires authors to be certain that what they write is true. Even if the author's intentions are innocent, if his statement can be reasonably interpreted as defamatory and it is false, he may find himself accused of—and worse, successfully sued for—libel. Similarly, if a statement can be reasonably interpreted to refer to a particular individual, it doesn't matter if the author actually intended it to refer to a different individual. (Authors, beware when writing about someone with a common name. Every individual named William Smith other than the particular William Smith you accused of thievery could, in theory, sue you for libel.) Even if you don't identify by name the person about whom you are writing, your words can still be deemed libelous. As long as a person can be reasonably identified, or misidentified, by your description of him or her, a jury will be free to decide that the statement was about that person.

Libel is not limited to individuals; legal entities, such as corporations and partnerships, can also be defamed, as can groups of people, although the group in question must be small enough that what is said can be reasonably assumed to be about particular, identifiable individuals. For example, a statement that the teachers in a local high school are unqualified for their jobs may be libelous if there are only ten of them but may not be libelous if there are a hundred of them.

By contrast, you can pretty much say what you want to say about dead people. States in general have no interest in protecting anybody's interest in a deceased person's good name.

In addition to statements about dead people, you may be able to get away with false and defamatory statements of opinion, which, no matter how wrongheaded, are protected by the First Amendment. But the line between fact and opinion is often fuzzy. Is saying someone is dishonest a statement of fact or of opinion? How about a statement that someone is a racist or an anti-Semite? (Answer in Pennsylvania: A statement that a public official is racist is fact, but a statement that he is anti-Semitic is opinion. Go figure.) Generally, if a statement cannot be verified as either true or false, it is an opinion. Opinions that seem to suggest the speaker knows facts to support them, however, may be treated as statements of fact—for example, a police officer expressing doubt about a woman's report of rape.

Some statements are so outlandish that they cannot be reasonably interpreted as statements of fact and therefore cannot be said to harm a person's reputation. Who would believe them? This reasoning famously led to the dismissal of Jerry Falwell's libel case against *Hustler* magazine for the statement, among others, that he had had sex with his mother. Conclusion: If you are going to libel someone, exaggerate!

Public officials, as well as those we consider public figures, are required by the First Amendment to grow thick skins. While you may be liable to a private individual simply for making a false and defamatory statement about him, liability to a public official or figure is limited to instances in which the author knows or has reason to believe that his statements are false. The courts describe making a statement with such knowledge as writing with "actual malice," which has nothing to do with how you feel about the person about whom you are making the statement, but everything to do with your intent to harm the target of your statement with its content.

This type of libel involves a host of legal questions: Who

qualifies as a public figure? What conduct demonstrates "actual malice"? What circumstances should lead a writer to believe that something is false? These all are topics that have been discussed, but not resolved, in pages and pages of legal opinions. It is enough to know that if you find yourself in this territory, you are in serious need of a lawyer.

While we're on the subject of hiring lawyers, keep in mind that being sued for libel can be very expensive, even aside from the cost of a lawyer to represent you. A person who has been defamed is entitled to be compensated for the harm to his reputation, as well as for what amounts to his "pain and suffering." Because such harm is impossible to measure, juries are free to compensate for these harms in whatever amount they find reasonable. Punitive damages can also be awarded to both private and public figures if the jury concludes the libelous statements were made with actual malice.

All this means that it is safest to write about dead people, next safest to write about public officials and public figures, and safest of all to write only the truth.

Evolution of the Genre

We have several ways to tell this story. A popular place to begin is in the 1960s, when a group of hardworking reporters and magazine writers began to chafe under the normal restrictions of journalistic writing. They started to break the rules. Writers like Joan Didion, Gay Talese, Lillian Ross, Tom Wolfe, and Hunter S. Thompson embraced a much more personal voice, no longer camouflaging the narrator's personality. They cultivated the subjective voice, believing that the writer's point of view had become an integral part of any story. Novelists also turned their hand to writing nonfiction and incorporated the narrative techniques that had served them so well in fiction. In 1966 Truman Capote examined the murder of a family in Kansas in his seminal work *In Cold Blood*. A few years later Norman Mailer's nonfiction meditation on an antiwar rally at the Pentagon became *The Armies of the Night*, a work that won a Pulitzer Prize. Its subtitle, *History as a Novel, the Novel as History*, spoke to the crossing of two great currents as journalism met creative writing. A new genre, often referred to as New Journalism, began to emerge in American letters.

Another starting point would be to look back into the mirror of literary history. Quickly we can locate a long tradition of creative nonfiction writings that lead in a direct line to the New Journalists of the twentieth century. We can find fascinating writing in Daniel Defoe's *The Storm*, his researched account of the great hurricane that struck Britain in 1703. James Boswell's *The Life of Samuel Johnson* (1791) offers a powerful profile of the inimitable literary figure that still teaches biographers of today how to write. Notable authors like Walt Whitman, Charles Dickens, Stephen Crane, and Jack London all began to explore using narrative techniques in their nonfiction reportage during the next century. George Orwell, Ernest Hemingway, John Steinbeck, James Agee, and Martha Gellhorn also explored nonfiction in their work while the *New Yorker* began a great tradition of featuring notable nonfiction, publishing A. J. Liebling, Joseph Mitchell, and E. B. White.

A third way to look at creative nonfiction's evolution is to look even earlier toward classical writers like Plutarch, Tacitus, and Herodotus. Their prose works reported on their world and times with grace and scholarship. Meditative essayists like Michel de Montaigne began a long tradition of thoughtful contemplative writing that examines the interior world of the author. Over time we can see a blending of the objective voice with the subjective.

Like any living art form, creative nonfiction continues to develop and deepen. Using a broad brushstroke to describe the genre's current trends, we can note a strong journalistic component in many nonfiction writers. These writers bring with them a long tradition of strict journalistic ethics, a commitment to reportage and a series of publishing venues (newspapers, magazines, and electronic media) that hold the same values. In the universities, a second thread is developing. Poets and fiction writers are producing lyrical essays and memoirs, emphasizing distinctly unjournalistic modes of storytelling. While they bring great narrative craft to their writings, they do not necessarily stress the journalistic demands for fact-based narrative.

If our theme is the evolution of a literary genre, it's helpful to look at the tenets of natural selection and how certain qualities or attributes help a species survive over time. Creative nonfiction is thriving yet moving in two different directions simultaneously. It will be interesting to see what develops next.

Facts

Facts such as statistics, numbers, and demographic data, the kind of information derived from mundane legwork, research, and scholarship, are the roots of creative nonfiction; they constitute the important teaching element, the informational content introduced throughout the story that leads to the reader's sense of discovery.

Defamed for simply providing information, facts are the underdogs of creative nonfiction. In reality, facts build upon and enhance the overall narrative structure, supplying tensile strength and depth to whatever true story is being told. Once the primary research is conducted and completed, the writer must examine the facts and figure out how to bind them together in such a way that an interesting, intellectual core can also be created as part of the narrative.

Ursula K. Le Guin reminded writers to "keep the story full," and though she was discussing fiction, we can apply her advice to creative nonfiction as well. Of course it's a given; no creative nonfiction writer (or reader) wants unprocessed facts piled on top of the writing with a snow shovel. Only the relevant facts and details belong; including everything can cause a story to lose focus. Relevant facts, as they apply to the strictly informational content of any piece of creative nonfiction, should be smoothly integrated into the story.

In *Coming into the Country*, John McPhee tells how he and two other men, on a hike in the Alaskan wilderness, see a grizzly bear. McPhee asks the two other men what will happen if the bear catches their scent. "We'd be in big trouble," replies the first man. "You can't outrun them," adds the second. McPhee follows up this brief conversation with these facts, which make the threat clear: "A grizzly, no slower than a race horse, is about half again as fast as the fastest human being. Watching the great mound of weight in the blueberries, with a fifty-five-inch waist and a neck more than thirty inches around, I had difficulty imagining that he could move at such speed, but I believed it and was without impulse to test the proposition."

Good, old-fashioned research and scholarship, either through immersion in a chosen subject à la John McPhee or through traditional print and electronic sources, are inescapable parts of a literary occupation. Yet creative nonfiction writers, especially beginners, often consider fact collecting and information gathering to be nothing more than the drudgery that must get done: the piles of handwritten index cards stacked on the card table; the color-coded file folders stuffed with assorted facts; the scraps of random details recorded on the pages of journals. All kept, but for what?

Still, writers like John McPhee hang on to those "useless" factoids and half-forgotten notes culled from a variety of scholarly and personal sources, for they may come to life later in unexpected ways.

Here, then, is a little discussed, mostly unacknowledged facet of facts: Facts hold creative power and possibility.

Alan Lightman, the author of *Einstein's Dreams* and an MIT

professor, says, "A prepared mind immersed in the facts and research comes before the creative moment."

Creative nonfiction writers, like scientists, cannot give up on the rigors of scholarship and factual immersion. We should welcome learning facts about the physical world, history, politics, birds, Celtic mythology—whatever we're interested in. From those very humble, underappreciated facts we read or personally observe, ideas and stories and metaphors may be born.

By staying close to the informational, journalistic roots of creative nonfiction, by simply hanging out in the world and paying close attention, we may find that a large chunk of that mundane fact collecting and routine research will lead to untold stories and to places that we, as writers and as readers, didn't know we could go.

Fact-checking

The James Frey scandal may have made the largest headlines in 2006, but Frey is far from the only writer who has duped the public. Take the case of Nasdijj, a prizewinning Navajo author who was unveiled by *LA Weekly* just a month or so after the Smoking Gun outed Frey. Over the past six years, "Nasdijj" (in reality a white man and an erstwhile penner of pornography, named Tim Barrus) wrote three best-selling memoirs: *The Blood Runs like a River through My Dreams*; *The Boy and the Dog Are Sleeping*; and *Geronimo's Bones: A Memoir of My Brother and Me*. As was the case with Frey, Nasdijj's publishers were warned by highly credible sources, including the Native American writer Sherman Alexie, that Nasdijj was likely a fake.

Why do companies such as Houghton Mifflin, Nasdijj's publisher, fail to fact-check? Why is the book publishing industry so indisposed to follow the example set by magazine and newspaper publishers, who generally verify all information before press time?

"Fact-checking in magazines is what makes the publication trustworthy in the eyes of the reader," says Sarah Z. Wexler, a freelance fact-checker who has worked for magazines like

Ladies' Home Journal and *GQ*. "People know that when they read a certain magazine, it's not just the writer's name they can trust but the magazine's name too. And the way the magazine keeps its name is by not making mistakes."

Unlike book publishing houses, magazines and newspapers keep regular staffs who treat fact-checking as their sole responsibility. The process is painstaking and important. "Almost all fact-checking is done over the phone," says Wexler. "You can try to compare information with other things that are published, but even then, that's not enough proof for another magazine to accept it as fact."

Writers are asked to provide sources that fact-checkers can double-check with, but the hours still add up. "Anything having to do with the military or any other large, bureaucratic organization is really tough because whomever you talk to usually has to get approval from somebody else above him," says Wexler, who once had to call more than fifteen people for a piece about military cowardice simply to confirm that the military had "no comment" on the subject, even though everyone knew this would be the answer.

For this reason, publishing houses claim that the profit margins on books simply do not allow for fact-checking budgets. Typical publishing companies issue hundreds or even thousands of nonfiction books a year. To fact-check each of these would be costly.

In addition, some writers object to the fact-checking of books, though for artistic rather than financial reasons. If memoirists were limited, for instance, to telling only those stories that could be independently verified by fact-checkers, many books might never make it to the shelf.

But other writers find solace in fact-checking. The fact-checker Wexler, who has also written for *Ladies' Home Journal*, sees the advantage of having the book-publishing industry change. "Part of what supports the writer is not just his name but . . . the publishing house. James Frey was hung out to dry. The publisher just has to say the author lied to them. I would feel more confident writing for a magazine, because at least you have the magazine's support behind you as a writer."

Family Members as Characters

In his popular memoir *Dress Your Family in Corduroy and Denim*, David Sedaris analogizes his work as a memoirist to that of a garbageman discarding the family trash: The job stinks. Sedaris writes that his sister Tiffany has become afraid to share any anecdotes from her life for fear that she will end up in his stories, being judged by him. "In this country, once something's out of your mouth, it's garbage," she quips as they ride toward her ramshackle apartment. Later, while his sister is preoccupied, Sedaris compulsively cleans the garbage out of her kitchen sink: "I fill the sink with hot, soapy water, roll up my shirtsleeves and start saving her life." It is clear that Sedaris does not have his sister's permission to "pick up" her garbage or examine the elements of her life that she would rather keep hidden. The author is doing exactly what his sister asks him not to do: He is making judgments about her life and attempting to alter it and, given the popularity of his work, is doing so on a rather public stage.

Indeed, Sedaris's family members may have particular reason to be wary of him: After an investigation of the truth behind Sedaris's stories, Alex Heard concluded in the *New Republic*: "Sedaris exaggerates too much for a writer using the nonfiction label." As for "whether David's exaggerations about family members ever amounted to fiction and whether this had caused any problems," Heard writes, "Not surprisingly, the occasional spark has crackled, with [his father] once telling the Raleigh paper, '[David's siblings] are really being invaded, you know, when he writes about them.'" For the most part, however, Heard suggests, Sedaris's family has made their peace with his stories; Sedaris's father, for example, "takes hard hits in the stories but seems unscarred."

Being related to a successful writer demands resilience and can even bring unexpected rewards. In an introduction to the tenth anniversary edition of *The Liars' Club*, Mary Karr writes about exposing her family's stories: "As certain facts that had once scalded all our insides and almost decimated our clan got broadcast a thousand times, we got oddly used to them. Call it aversion therapy, but the events seeped in a little deeper. We healed more—though that had never been the point—through exposure." The act of publishing family drama can thus be simultaneously selfish and altruistic.

Too, in his defense, Sedaris remarks in *Dress Your Family in Corduroy and Denim* that there is a distinct ethical difference between someone's offering you a perfectly good article of trash for reuse and stealing something out of a person's garbage can without his or her permission, though in the case of family, it's not always clear which category research falls into. A writer who interviews a public figure, notebook and tape recorder in hand, is clearly researching a story, and the subject should consider himself warned; it is harder to maintain constant wariness toward a brother. Should family members of writers have to censor their dinner conversations for fear of finding them reproduced and dissected in a book?

Perhaps inevitably, nonfiction writers who use members of

their families as their subjects reveal information that the families would prefer to keep private. For this reason, writers' use of family members as subjects frequently affects their familial relationships and daily interactions.

Furthermore, there are always conflicting loyalties at work when nonfiction writers sit down to write about their families. No one can be completely objective about family; even the best of writers can grapple with vengeance, pride, and deep-rooted insecurities when writing about a relative.

Indeed, in some cases a writer's strong feelings about his family, even strongly negative feelings, can provide a great story, especially if the writer has inside access to information not available to scholars or other writers. In *Sweet and Low*, Rich Cohen dissects both his family and its artificial sweetener business. Cohen, who has been disinherited from the family, shamelessly investigates his relatives and writes an unflattering account of their public and private actions. Cohen clearly has little loyalty to his family and next to no respect for his relatives' privacy. But in a narrative that exposes many dirty secrets about how the moguls of the fake sugar industry came into power, these are not necessarily bad motivations to have. As a renounced heir Cohen hasn't got much to lose and therefore tells all.

Most writers don't have the arguable luxury of having been disinherited, however, so they have to be more careful about the stories they tell. In some cases, this means letting family members vet drafts of work and giving them veto power. Other writers publish memoirs thinly veiled as novels, though rarely is the veil thick enough to be convincing. But in any event, writers must think carefully about the value and consequences—because there almost certainly will be consequences—of turning their family members into characters.

Forewords and Afterwords

In an age when author fabrications have led to firings, forfeited Pulitzer Prizes, and vast reader distrust of a million little memoirs, conscientious nonfiction writers turn increasingly to forewords and afterwords to bring the reader behind the scenes of the work. Here writers can disclose the hurdles they faced, and the ethical and artistic choices they made, in both researching and reconstructing the story. In a foreword or afterword, a writer can try to shape the way the work will be read.

The author's note that opens *Schindler's List*, Thomas Keneally's best-selling 1982 volume, offers a model of a masterful foreword. Keneally describes how he stumbled onto Oskar Schindler's story during a 1980 visit to a Beverly Hills luggage store. There he met one of the twelve hundred Jews Schindler had rescued from the ghettos and transports of the Nazi death machine. Keneally describes the exhaustive research that undergirds his story: interviews with fifty Schindler rescuees; on-site visits with one of these survivors to the major locales of the tale; Schindler's papers and private letters; and written testimonies deposited by Schindler Jews at Yad Vashem, the Holocaust Martyrs' and Heroes' Remembrance Authority. Keneally then explains some of the choices he made and introduces the reader to one of his book's major themes, the complexity (and ambiguity) of heroism.

The afterword to *The Executioner's Song*, Norman Mailer's 1979 Pulitzer Prize–winning volume, achieves similar goals. Mailer describes the interviews, court transcripts, and other documents that permitted him to re-create the unsettling saga of Utah mass murderer Gary Gilmore, who wanted only to die. Mailer expresses humility (and protects himself) in this afterword, for Gilmore's firing squad death left the writer in the awkward plight of never having met his work's central figure. "This book does its best to be a factual account of the activities of Gary Gilmore and the men and women associated with him in the period from April 9, 1976, when he was released from the United States Penitentiary at Marion, Illinois, until his execution a little more than nine months later in Utah State Prison," Mailer begins—the sentence itself precise yet tempering. "[T] he story is as accurate as one can make it," he later declares, and then describes some of the obstacles he faced. When two accounts of the same episode differed, he chose the version that seemed most likely; however, the author acknowledges, speaking of himself in the third person, "It would be vanity to assume he was always right."

Which is better, a foreword or an afterword? Each site holds advantages and liabilities. The foreword spot is more prominent and may be more likely to be read than will an afterword, so writers might gravitate to the foreword if they have information to convey essential to proper reading of the text. Less vital background information, in contrast, might wait for an afterword. Some writers want to plunge the reader headlong into the story without pause for niceties; here too the afterword appeals.

Writers can communicate their choices to readers in smaller ways, should their works not lend themselves to a fore- or afterword. Truman Capote added a subtitle to *In Cold Blood: A True Account of a Multiple Murder and Its Consequences*. These ten words set the terms for the book's reading and evaluation. Agents, editors, and publishers can help writers form honorable contracts by truthful pitching, labeling, and marketing of works and by vigilant pursuit at the least hint of fabrication. Savvy readers today look eagerly for book labels and other clues. Those who wish to place themselves in the most knowing context to appreciate the work will rely on any foreword or afterword.

Frame

The plot of a story—the documented change in people, places, or objects—poses questions: What is happening? What has caused this to happen? And most important, how will it end? To keep the reader engaged, the writer must point in a specific direction, toward specific questions. It is the nonfiction writer's job to construct a story of actual events that poses a degree of suspense.

The building blocks of creative nonfiction are scenes, little stories, but scenes require some sort of order. One scene must follow another in a relatively clear pattern. That pattern, a story in itself, is called a frame.

A frame gives shape to a story and keeps readers reading in order to find out what happens. In between plot developments, the creative nonfiction writer can supply other information, tell other stories, and explore the themes that drive the story.

Consider an episode of the ubiquitous TV show *Law & Order*. It usually begins when a body is accidentally discovered: scene one. The detectives arrive and scope out the crime scene, sum up the circumstances of the murder. The veteran detective Lenny (Jerry Orbach, until just before he died in December 2004), usually ends this, scene two, with a funny or ironic comment.

The scenes go on, one after another, in a logical progression. Suspects are interviewed, released, and finally arrested. The district attorney's office takes over, and a trial ensues. More scenes. Tension. The frame, the overall plot, generally advances until at the end, the viewer learns whether the subject who is arrested and tried is convicted. All the scenes are, in other words, framed in a larger story.

Of course, frames need not advance in a beginning to end chronology. Writers can start a frame in the middle, as John McPhee does in his classic essay "Travels in Georgia," which begins with a scene in which he and two traveling companions, Sam and Carol, naturalists with the Georgia Natural Areas Council, discover a snapping turtle DOR—dead on the road—and scrape it off the highway with the intention of eating it for dinner. Shortly thereafter they arrive at the bank of a stream, where a dragline crane operator named Chap Causey is widening the riverbed.

McPhee and his companions are on a thirteen-hundred-mile ride through the state, examining wetlands and discussing the importance of conserving them as a habitat for wildlife. This scene with the crane gobbling up the riverbank is a stark illustration of what's at stake, so it provides a vivid and engaging beginning for the story. To be effective, a frame must reflect the focus of a story.

McPhee then loops back to the beginning of his journey. In the next twenty-five pages, nearly two-thirds of the story, he explains how he came to travel with Sam and Carol and develops them more fully as characters. They stop for more DORs and spend time at Carol's house with her menagerie of rescued animals and collection of animal bones. They camp out and eat DOR muskrat and paddle down a river in the moonlight.

Each of these scenes advances the story; they all are connected to its focus. We learn about Carol, for example, in myriad ways, but all of these are related to her passion for preserving Georgia's wetlands. An essay is more than a simple collection of terrific scenes and information, no matter how cleverly organized. Each part of the frame must have a specific emphasis or theme that relates to the larger story being told.

Finally, the narrative delivers McPhee and his companions back to the riverbank and Chap Causey's crane, and then McPhee moves on and finishes both his journey and his story, which end with a canoe ride and a conversation with a young Jimmy Carter, then governor of Georgia.

McPhee is a master of framing; other frames he has employed in stories include a tennis match ("Centre Court," in which a championship game between Arthur Ashe and Clark Graebner provides the opportunity to profile not only both men but the sport of tennis itself) and a Monopoly game ("The Search for Marvin Gardens," in which McPhee tours Atlantic City). Each of these frames offers the opportunity for a narrative that leads the reader but also provides space for other information.

Wherever a writer chooses to start his story, there must always be a way to order the scenes, a larger connecting story with a clear beginning and end.

Getting Inside Characters' Heads

The inner thoughts and feelings of characters appear regularly in fiction, but is the interior life fair game for the nonfiction writer as well? To put it bluntly, can a nonfiction writer convey with any confidence a person's inner thoughts and feelings at a particular moment in time? How can writers possibly *know*?

Many nonfiction writers believe they can access this inner world. They rest their claim on the many testimonials of an easily tested feat, that many people can recall not only their thoughts and feelings but often the very words exchanged in major moments: the winning basket; a marriage proposal; heartbreak; accident; loss. And many can summon the moment not just immediately afterward but across all their days.

Gay Talese believes interior reports and interior monologues can be useful tools for the nonfiction writer when wielded with care and finesse. For his 1964 *Esquire* profile of boxer Floyd Patterson, he wanted to give his readers access to an experience most would never know, what it feels like to be knocked out. By then Talese had written thirty-seven articles about the heavyweight fighter, each one representing at least one extended visit. He had lived with Patterson at his training camp and jogged beside him during roadwork. "I had become almost an interior figure in his life," Talese explains. "I was his second skin."

In the ironically titled "The Loser," Talese unfolds the longest direct quotation of his career. Patterson relived his second humiliating defeat at the hands of Sonny Liston, with Talese sitting at his side. "I felt at this moment like a witness to his private thoughts, a partner in his privacy with permission to write about this privacy," Talese recalls. "I was hearing, I felt, what echoes inside a man who feels absolutely alone."

Because Talese knew Patterson so well and had gained his trust, he was able at times to break into the fighter's reverie, sometimes to slow Patterson down, sometimes to push him deeper into himself. After describing the surprising euphoria he felt in the first seconds of the knockdown, Patterson began to pace and continued: "But then this good feeling leaves you. You realize where you are, and what you're doing there, and what has just happened to you. And what follows is a hurt, a confused hurt." Talese repeated the fighter's last words as a question: "A confused hurt?" This spurred Patterson to say: "Not a physical hurt—it's a hurt combined with anger; it's a what-will-people-think hurt." Again Talese softly queried: "A what-will-people-think hurt?" Patterson went deeper: "It's an ashamed-of-my-own-ability hurt." By using this gentle probing technique, Talese was actually going inside with his source. "I was helping him," he says. "I was also getting a more refined quote. He was not only going deeper, he was rewriting himself. This is a technique any interviewer can use."

Interior reports, like any technique, can be abused or overused. Writers can reduce mistakes, however, by spending time with their sources. Time reveals whether a person embellishes stories or makes self-serving remarks. Then the writer can decide how to use these interior reports or whether to use them at all.

Guiding the Reader

In Charleston, South Carolina, there is a tour guide who can show visitors stand-alone garages on back alleys that once served as slave quarters, point out street corners that figure prominently in Gershwin's *Porgy and Bess*, and sing, in a clear tenor voice, the calls of the street vendors in the opera.

A tour guide's job is a lot like the work nonfiction writers do. A good nonfiction book leads a reader on a journey, allowing her to discover parts of the world that she might not normally see. She may never orbit the earth in a rocket capsule, but she can read Tom Wolfe's *The Right Stuff* and learn something about that experience.

If a guide sings a bit of a Gershwin song, a writer like James Agee can quote the Lord's Prayer in *Let Us Now Praise Famous Men* with similar authority. Writers can decorate their writing with narrative devices, using scenes, dialogue, and other storytelling strategies. These literary techniques help elevate writing from formulaic prose to a complex narrative that surprises and delights.

Readers want to trust the narrator as a reliable witness, a source of authentic information. Tour guides operate under a similar dictate: In order to create a good tour, the guide must study history texts, guidebooks, and biographies and then incorporate some of that information into his script. This level of research helps convince people that their guide is trustworthy. The writer has tools as well; for example, setting off a conversation with quotation marks is a signal that someone actually spoke those words. Creative nonfiction's great literary power comes from its essential connection to fact. If writers compromise that relationship, the writing grows weaker, and they risk losing their audience.

Most important, the tour guide's role is to tell readers where to look. The filmmaker Akira Kurosawa reminds us that "to be an artist means never to avert one's eyes." John Hersey's *Hiroshima* opened American eyes to the disturbing realities of the atomic bomb by tracking six individuals' experiences from the time just before the bomb fell. In the process of following these characters through the aftermath of the bombing, Hersey effectively gave readers a tour of the devastated city. In creative nonfiction, the author takes the active stance of paying attention to the world and, as a witness, stays faithful to fact, pointing out what the reader must see.

Gunkholing: Finding a Story

Gunkholing is an old sailors' pastime; if the fish aren't biting, sailors sometimes pull their boats into secluded coves to cast and lower their nets in order to find what muck and materials lie on the ocean's floor. When creative nonfiction writers gunkhole, they too lower their nets, to learn more about what's beneath a subject's surface. At first a given topic may appear to have little to offer. But a good writer, through literary skill, impeccable research, and some mysterious, personal intuition, knows when to sound the depths.

One of the best-known examples of finding the story behind a story is Truman Capote's *In Cold Blood*. Capote's curiosity was first piqued while reading a *New York Times* story about a brutal small-town Kansas murder. As he read reports about the killers and the murders' horrible details, Capote had a sixth sense that there was more to the story. A deep emotional spark combined with his well-developed storytelling instincts, and Capote set off for Kansas. He spent months at a time there, developing relationships with the murderers and other key players, to try to gain a more direct perspective rather than a distant, abstract one.

Tracy Kidder's book *House* is another good example of how

a writer can take what appears to be a rather mundane topic, a story about the design and construction of a single-family house, and make it come alive. Kidder doesn't just describe the ins and outs of how a custom house is built; he weaves a dramatic story. Readers learn about the personalities, obsessions, and dreams of everyone involved, from the workers to the owners. "I started out writing about carpenters, a history, but I realized the house was an incredible intersection of social, historical and economic concerns," Kidder told the *New York Times* in 1985. "The idea was to take a small thing and see what's emblematic in it." A similar instinct, perhaps, has in recent years led many writers to what Adam Gopnik, in the *New Yorker*, called "little-thing/big-thing books," books about subjects including salt, nutmeg, and the color mauve.

It's all in the execution; any subject matter can be made interesting in creative nonfiction. Besides collecting general information, reading all the background literature, talking to any people directly or indirectly involved in the potential story, and paying careful, close attention as all good writers do, a creative nonfiction writer will always ask: Is there something more here? In the beginning, when tinkering around to focus a topic, a writer may not be able to answer easily or readily the critical question, Who cares? That's when it's time to pull into the cove and gunkhole for a while; one of the most important tasks in creative nonfiction is to search until the unseen but essential treasures in any potential subject are truly and wondrously brought to life.

History into Nonfiction Narrative

Historians have always crafted narratives. War. Peace. Political battles. Feuds in the hollers. Floods on the Mississippi. Hurricanes. Strikes. Assassinations. Voyages to known and unknown places. Trials of the century. Personal quests. Leaders with uncommon touches and tragic flaws. This is the stuff of great narrative and the stuff of narrative history, stories about the past told with verve and drama but also with strong arguments and thick footnotes.

Over the years historians—and here we're talking largely about American university-trained and -based scholars—have produced numerous libraries' worth of moving tales spiced with telling details set against carefully drawn backdrops and built around scrupulously fleshed-out characters. Just like any good nonfiction instructor, Samuel Eliot Morison, one of the twentieth century's most brilliant and widely read historians, urged his Harvard graduate students to read more than academic books and journals. According to a recent article in the *New Yorker*, Morison told them to study the art of the novel and the grace of the essay. He feared that without this grounding his students would write only "dull, solid" monographs. Morison wasn't a self-loathing historian, just a realistic one. Each "dull, solid" book and article, he knew, added to the base of historical knowledge, but that was it. No one outside the small cohort of scholars in a subfield would ever read them. For most historians, this was OK. Tenure and promotion come through deeply researched accounts of wars, trials, and political campaigns targeted at other academics, not through broadly conceived narratives aimed at large audiences.

The scope of the historical profession narrowed a bit more in the 1960s and 1970s. Borrowing techniques and approaches from social scientists, historians churned out streams of studies tightly focused on the daily lives of ordinary, often forgotten people and on long-term patterns of work, mobility, and reproduction that showcased method, data sets, and argument over plot, suspense, and character development. Fearful that the hints of play and performance that came with narrative would take away from the veracity and seriousness of the accounts, some deliberately shied away from artful storytelling. Better in this professional climate to construct tables and long, discursive footnotes than chiseled characters and in-depth scenes.

Journalists, features writers, and biographers quickly stepped into the narrative void left by the historians' social-scientific turn. Skilled storytellers and diligent researchers like J. Anthony Lukas and Robert A. Caro told gripping tales of race and disappointment, city building and power brokers. Audiences came running. David McCullough recounted the building of the Brooklyn Bridge, and John Barry traced the floodwaters of the Mississippi, and readers turned the pages. Doris Kearns Goodwin and Stephen Ambrose (Ambrose started out as a university-based historian but chafed under the academy's narrative and political constraints, or so he said) retold sprawling national narratives of good and evil, and book buyers swarmed. Taylor

Branch and Edmund Morris buried themselves in the archives and produced gripping, authoritative accounts of the lives of Martin Luther King, Jr., and Teddy Roosevelt, and the scribes of the *New York Review of Books* debated their insights.

Just as Samuel Morison had predicted, strong writers of compelling narratives had, by the 1980s, taken over the popular market for history. Unwilling to concede the past to nonprofessionals, some historians looked to strike back. But they knew that this meant rediscovering their field's deep narrative traditions. It meant taking on the big topics. It also meant imitating the narrative strategies deployed so well by journalist-historians like Goodwin and Caro—with, of course, fatter footnotes and longer bibliographies.

Reflecting the trend, in 1989 Princeton Professor James M. McPherson crafted *Battle Cry of Freedom*, a vivid, even moving account of the military history of the Civil War. In the following decade Joseph Ellis, of Mount Holyoke College, published *American Sphinx*, an elegant look at the private Thomas Jefferson. This triggered a sort of founding fathers revival, as professors, this time with the journalists following, raced to see who would get out the next book on Hamilton, Jefferson, or Adams. Others who missed this bandwagon turned their attention to Lincoln and the noble grunts of World War II. As these accounts started to appear on the *New York Times*' Best Sellers list, other historians hired agents and looked to capture a slice of this growing audience. But even more, the renewed interest in narrative, and the royalty checks, trickled down. Graduate programs from Princeton to North Carolina to Southern California started to offer writing seminars alongside methods classes, featuring the work of Lukas and McPherson as well as of Gay Talese and Philip Roth.

But the grand narrative of the big event and the big leader wasn't the only thing happening in the history business. The freedom movements of the 1960s rocked the academy. African Americans, women, Native Americans, Chicanos, gays, lesbians, and transgendered people demanded not just equity before the law but also a place in the nation's past. Yet including the "others" upset some firmly established master narratives. Things weren't so clear anymore. Whose story was true? historians wondered. The answer depended on the perspective.

Some historians concluded, with great misgivings, that truth was subjective. It wasn't that there wasn't truth but that truth—the past—looked different depending on where one stood. For some, this insight brought liberation from the restrictions of the omnipresent third-person narrative, the detached and commanding position adopted by historians. Some scholars then began to experiment with voice and structure. With a novelist's eye for detail and phrasing, James E. Goodman, in *Stories of Scottsboro*, retells the tragedy of the wrongly accused Scottsboro boys from a multiplicity of angles with each chapter changing perspective. In his following book, *Blackout*, an account of the night the lights went out in New York City in 1977, he retells the event in a frenzy of more than fifty short story blasts. The complexity of experience is what matters to him.

Others have injected themselves into their stories. Art historian Eunice Lipton went searching for Manet's model in *Alias Olympia* and found herself. In *Blood Done Sign My Name*, Timothy B. Tyson recalled a racially charged murder in his southern hometown to reinterpret the civil rights movement and the politics of his minister father. And John Demos, a Yale professor and highly respected colonial historian, ran into some dead ends in the archives, but rather than give up his stories, he imagined his way into the heads of his characters, writing brief fictions as history in *The Unredeemed Captive.*

Creative nonfiction writers have been slow to pick up on historians' narrative experiments. But this adventurous spirit, and perhaps some advice about conducting research, are among historians' most valuable offerings. Truth is precarious, unstable, and elusive, and this, as Goodman, Demos, and the others show, is the real drama of the past. The search for truth, the battle for whose truth matters and what truth gets codified into official histories, textbooks, and monuments, is the stuff of stories—tense, suspenseful stories—the stuff of both creative nonfiction and narrative history.

The "I"

Ursula K. Le Guin may have coined the most succinct description of the character called I that's constructed on the page: "I am an artist . . . and therefore a liar. Distrust everything I say. I am telling the truth." The first sentence establishes the primary identity of the "I" and describes her reason for her self-examination; the second sentence declares that the "I" is unreliable and shows that the author is aware of and open about her unreliability; and the third lets the reader know that her examination of her unreliability is a tool that allows her to illustrate better the truth of herself, her purpose, her story. It is the combination of the last two statements that helps the author earn her reader's trust. But all three elements are necessary when developing a reflective piece of creative nonfiction.

Sandell Morse uses all three elements in "Canning Jars," which describes an encounter with an anti-Semitic antiques dealer while Morse day-tripped with a friend in Virginia. Morse and the salesman haggle over the price of a set of glass canning jars that she hopes to purchase as Hanukkah gifts for her sons. Morse smiles as they agree on a price. But the salesman does not smile:

. . . I'm not prepared for what he says, can't believe
I'm hearing it correctly. I lean in. His words slur.
Understanding seeps, slowly, so slowly that he must
repeat. "I hate a woman Jew."
     The blow is swift, rushing quickly into my stom-
ach where revulsion and fear swirl in a vortex. . . .
I want to move but I can't. I feel rooted and mute,
and I wonder: Does he see a telltale sign? Smell an
odor? . . .
     I wonder if I've done something wrong—played
the game incorrectly, been too cheap, should've
gone up. And so I take what it is that is happening
here in this room into my gut where it opens up old
wounds. . . .

In her portrayal of this scene Morse has to avoid re-creating
her subjects, the salesman and herself, as clichéd characters.
If she portrays herself as a perfect character who is not self-
critical or self-reflective or as a victim who is self-righteous, or
if she simply portrays the salesman as a monster, she will lose
the brutal complexity of the fact that this is an ordinary man, a
quiet shop, a sunny day and that she is an ordinary woman, full
of faults and self-doubts. But by describing her own process of
handling the crisis and questioning her individual response to
the ancient fear she bears, Morse encourages the reader to trust
the writer's ability to critique and evaluate her own actions as
well as the actions of her nemesis. She constructs her persona
through reflection.
     In an interview, Morse reflected on her process of "research-
ing" herself in order to create her narration for "Canning Jars,"
using the terms "I" and "eye" to discuss the dual function of an

author in a personal essay. The latter term describes Morse's ability to show the reader what she is witnessing, to allow the reader to see through her eyes as if they were camera lenses. The former term depicts the author's actions and mediations, as if a camera were trained on them. Morse also discussed the function and construction of a nonfiction narrator: "We must remember that the 'I' (eye) of creative nonfiction is a persona," she said. "The 'I' of one essay is not the 'I' of another."

As Morse and Le Guin point out, the function of the "I" within creative nonfiction tends to be different from that of the "I" of journalism, whose primary tasks are usually narration and argument and who tends not to have a life or story of his or her own. Writers of creative nonfiction have more space to question the biases, actions, and intentions of the "I" within a piece, while still maintaining authorial control over their stories and conveying information. As a result, both writer and reader learn more about what it means to be and to study the "I."

Immersion

The dark bar smells of decades of cigarette smoke. The Mexicans gathered at the table are desperate, poor, and about to risk all they have to cross the border into the United States. Ted Conover tells this story in his book *Coyotes: A Journey through the Secret World of America's Illegal Aliens*. To research this book, Conover posed as an immigrant for a year, crossing the U.S.-Mexican border four times and traveling through various states with migrant workers, picking lemons and oranges alongside them.

Conover used a technique known as immersion, a practice that goes back to George Plimpton's *Paper Lion* and Henry David Thoreau's *Walden*. The writer submerges himself in his subject, allowing his quest for the story to take over his life. Plimpton, for example, spent a season in training camp with the Detroit Lions. Some writers spend years researching their subjects in this painstaking way. But the intimate details and thorough understanding that result make immersion worth the effort. "I believe in immersion in the events of a story," writes Tracy Kidder, the Pulitzer Prize-winning author of *The Soul of a New Machine*, *House*, *Home Town*, and many other books. "I take it on faith that the truth lies in the events somewhere and that immersion in those real events will yield glimpses of that truth."

Successful immersion often demands that the writer's presence be as unobtrusive as possible, and some writers go to great lengths to blend in. To understand the lives of American men, *Los Angeles Times* columnist Norah Vincent worked out to add fifteen pounds of bulk to her shoulders, wore a cupless sports bra, glued on facial stubble made of wool crepe paste, and sported a flattop, rectangular glasses, and rugby shirts. According to a review in the *New York Times*, the resulting book, *Self-Made Man*, "transcends its premise altogether, offering not an undercover woman's take on male experience but simply a fascinating, fly-on-the-wall look at various unglamorous male milieus that are well off the radar of most journalists and book authors."

Such drastic action is not always necessary, however; writers such as Kidder and John McPhee manage to minimize their presence during immersion without resorting to disguises. McPhee, in particular, is known for disappearing into the background, not only while reporting but also in the resulting stories, employing the first-person pronoun only when reporting scenes that take place in situations (on a canoe trip, in a small airplane) that would seem odd if written without an acknowledgment of the author's presence.

Of course, as Conover's experience illustrates, being completely invisible is often impossible. Conover has blond hair, blue eyes, and an Amherst education, and he admits that his presence probably changed what happened when the Mexicans were caught on the border and how they spoke to one another in his presence. Conover himself was part of the story, and so when writing, he decided the third person would not do. He stuck out in that bar as no fly would, and thus he had to use the personal pronoun "I." It was the honest thing to do.

Although Conover may not have had much of a choice, writers can keep their influence to a minimum during immersion by limiting their interaction with subjects. Lee Gutkind, in *The Art of Creative Nonfiction*, suggests that for many writers, "the tendency is to find a place for yourself and to help out in order to make yourself be and feel useful. This approach does not usually work well. . . . For a writer, sitting, watching and taking the occasional note is a key and vital activity. If you are helping the people you are observing on a regular basis, then you are not writing. If you are perceived as part of the team, then you are not perceived as a writer, a misconception that may lead to misunderstandings down the line."

How can a writer know when the immersion process is over? Gutkind advises that you hang in with your first round of immersion until you can think of no more questions to ask. After writing your first draft, you'll see where the gaps lie in your research, which will force you to go back into immersion for more material. "I usually will go back three or four times until my essay or book seems complete," says Gutkind.

Influencing Readers

Great creative nonfiction does not shirk from controversial topics or sometimes from passing judgment on them. After all, writers become fully engaged in their subjects and inevitably come to conclusions about them, and often they will want readers to share these conclusions. But in terms of craft, confronting contentious topics, passing judgment on them, and persuading readers to follow along require great skill. Writers must strive for just the right tone (jaded? angry? bemused? objective?), a carefully constructed (but often subtle) thesis, and a conclusion (again, often subtle) backed by logic and evidence.

Writers who are skilled at persuasion have ancient forebears; the dictates of persuasion date all the way back to Aristotle and have changed little over the past two millennia. And while one imagines Aristotle might not have fully appreciated gonzo journalism, a manic, highly subjective form of reportage that originated in the seventies, the father of gonzo, Hunter S. Thompson, was also a master of persuasion.

The author's notorious, drug-fueled antics aside, Thompson's work is characterized by a clear, logical, and precise mind. A full arsenal of persuasive tools is on display in one of his earliest forays into gonzo, "The Temptations of Jean-Claude Killy," originally published in 1970. Killy, an Olympic skier, was one of the first Olympic athletes to develop a relationship with corporate sponsors. While Killy's character is the focus of the essay, the piece is really a critique of the commercialization of sports. It came at a time when many sportswriters were unwilling to confront this issue and Thompson's willingness to assert that commercialization corrupted athletes and made their lives miserable was significant and cutting-edge.

Throughout "Temptations," Thompson leads readers a little closer to his argument each time he describes Killy's promoting another product, allowing the athlete's actions and speech to convey the falsity and high cost of his selling out. Thompson cleverly employs some classic techniques from the art of persuasion. He carefully establishes the debate's key focus at the essay's beginning, praises Killy to maintain an air of objectivity, and employs a barrage of evidence to convince readers that the Olympian has fallen from grace.

Thompson starts his essay not with his first meeting with Killy but when he meets a friend at the Boston airport. He tells his friend he wants to have a drink with him instead of sticking with Killy's entourage: "I've been chasing all over the country for 10 days on this thing: Chicago, Denver, Aspen, Salt Lake City, Sun Valley, Baltimore. . . . I'm supposed to ride up [to New Hampshire] with them tonight . . . but I'm not up to it; all those hired geeks with their rib-ticklers."

Thompson's complaint to his friend also registers with readers, extending friendship to them too. And because the complaints are based on ten days of real experience, readers are more likely to tolerate them. In fact, Thompson has carefully constructed the narrative to take the reader on a roller-coaster ride of inductive reasoning, lining up each particular piece of evidence to support his conclusion that Killy is corrupt.

Next, Thompson expresses his admiration for Killy's athleticism, a step that is likely to win favor with readers and also establishes Thompson's fairness toward his subject. Then, with the requisite admiration logged in, Thompson begins to chip away at Killy, his careful verbal jabs like a series of perfectly administered karate chops. Over breakfast, Killy turns pitchman with a press release that he has received from Chevrolet about a rise in sales. "I looked to see if he was smiling," Thompson writes, "but his face was deadly serious and his voice was pure snake oil."

To reestablish his credibility and fairness, Thompson again backs off to admire Killy, the athlete: "Killy's whole secret is his feverish concentration. He attacks a hill like Sonny Liston used to attack Floyd Patterson—and with the same kind of awesome results. He wants to beat the hill, not just ski it." Throughout the rest of the narrative, however, Thompson allows Killy to hang himself (in one beautifully rendered scene, Killy snaps at a little girl who is trying to take his picture) until the reader is overwhelmed with the athlete's loutishness. By the end of the piece Thompson has freed himself to express his contempt for Killy openly.

Thompson's method follows the approach laid out by Aristotle, who identified the ways in which the psychology of readers and writers interacts and how an emotional appeal (in Aristotelian terms, pathos) is a necessary element of persuasion. But emotion can't stand on its own; the interaction between writer and reader is dependent upon ethos, or the character of the writer (much like developing the right tone or persona).

Logos, Aristotle's third element of persuasion, refers to the quality of the argument itself.

Most writers have a pretty good idea of how they want their readers to respond to their work emotionally and intellectually, whether the work is a memoir about an abusive ex-spouse, a carefully researched essay about an art heist, or a tale of a fishing boat lost at sea. Getting the reader to follow along is the real trick. But by keeping the three elements of persuasion in mind—ethos, pathos, and particularly logos—writers can be sure that their work contains the necessary elements not only to move and compel their readers but to lead them to agree with the writers' conclusions.

Keeping It Brief

"Anybody can have ideas—the difficulty is to express them without squandering a quire of paper on an idea that ought to be reduced to one glittering paragraph." That's Mark Twain, arguing against verbosity.

Twain would likely have been a fan of the nonfiction short.

Taking a page from the popularity of sudden fiction, editors Judith Kitchen and Mary Paumier Jones put brief nonfiction on the literary map with their 1996 anthology *In Short*. In their introduction, Kitchen and Jones attribute the trend toward brevity in part to writers and readers "schooled by the quick takes of television and the movies" translating a rapid grasp of scene and context to the written word.

In an introduction to the collection (so popular it was followed by a second, *In Brief*, and a third, *Short Takes*), Bernard Cooper, author of *Maps to Anywhere*, suggests that short nonfiction "requires an alertness to detail, a quickening of the senses, a focusing of the literary lens, so to speak, until one has magnified some small aspect of what it means to be human."

Cooper is among the contemporary essayists who focus on brief nonfiction. Others include Eduardo Galeano, Stuart Dybek, Brian Doyle, and Abigail Thomas, author of *Safekeep-*

ing, an engaging memoir made up of one- and two-page chapters, some as brief as one hundred words. The very concise form seems to attract a fair share of poets, and in fact, the border between sudden nonfiction and the prose poem remains murky and under dispute.

Kitchen and Jones, in their three anthologies, define "brief" as "2,000 words or less," a challenge to many writers accustomed to a wider canvas, but the online journal *Brevity* takes an even stingier approach, limiting writers to 750 words.

Brevity editor Dinty W. Moore asks his writers for sharp description and careful distillation. "I like to imagine a brush fire, deep inside a national park," he explains. "The reader is a firefighter, and the writer's job is to parachute that reader directly to the edge of the blaze to encounter flame and smoke immediately. There is no time for the long hike in."

Legal Responsibilities of Publishers

One of the hardest things for people to understand about libel law is that publishers are legally as liable as writers are. Even if the publishing company clearly states, in a disclaimer at the front of a memoir or a newspaper editorial, that someone else is the author of the statement and the publisher is not endorsing the statement as true, the publisher has an obligation to print only the truth.

Take the case of a politician who issues a press release accusing her opponent of taking illegal bribes. A newspaper reporter receives the press release and consequently writes a story reporting the politician's allegation about her opponent. The newspaper publishes the reporter's story. (It is news after all.) If the allegation is false, the politician and the reporter as well as the newspaper all may be sued successfully for libel, depending on the circumstances. For this reason, a publisher's responsibility for the statements that appear in his newspapers, magazines, and books or on their Web pages is exactly the same as the author's. This is why some publishers hire fact-checkers.

Employing fact-checkers to review information before it is published is one way for publishers to show that they've taken precautions against acting negligently. Publishers may not be able to avoid being sued for libel, but they may be able to defend themselves against big money judgments in the case of rulings against them by taking the reasonable precautions that will enable them to prove in court that even if what they printed was false and defamatory, it certainly was not published with actual malice.

Publishers can also avoid lawsuits by employing common sense and carefully reading everything submitted for publication. Some things just do not make sense. Some things stretch our credulity. Some things are internally inconsistent or inconsistent with other facts we know to be true. When a nonsensical, incredible, or inconsistent piece of writing also defames an identifiable living person, the publisher should ask hard questions of the author and refuse to print the writing until his questions have been answered satisfactorily. Otherwise, the publisher may be printing a piece with actual malice—that is, with a reason to know that it may not be true. (A great deal hinges on actual malice. In the case of writing about public figures, it is the standard for liability; in the case of private individuals, proof of actual malice allows for the recovery of punitive damages.)

A publisher cannot turn a blind eye to suspicious "facts." If it is possible to verify whether something is true or not—by checking a public record, for example—a publisher must do so. He may not know that a particular fact is false, but if he could have found out that it was false, he might still be in trouble.

The same procedures should be followed for vetting every article. Failure to follow the established protocol for an article that turns out to be false and defamatory may help prove negligence and may also be evidence of actual malice. There is of course no official journalistic code, but to the extent that there is a set of generally accepted industry standards, publishers should follow them—not least because experts will be called on to testify about their existence in court.

Publishers (and, by extension, authors) must be especially wary of negative statements that are written about a person who is not a public official or figure because the plaintiff's burden of proof in such cases is less stringent. Writers can be held liable even if all they do is repeat what others have said, even if the "others" are the police or other public officials. If, for example, a detective says a suspect is a rapist and a writer prints that statement, the suspect must actually be a rapist in order for the writer and publisher to escape liability for repeating the statement. (Hence the frequent use of the word "alleged" in news reports.)

Further complications arise when an author relies on unnamed sources in his article or book. The author swears the source is reliable, but how can the publisher know? Unless the publisher knows the source has proved reliable in the past, he may not be able to protect himself from a libel suit. At the very least, the publisher should know how the source knows what he purports to know and be convinced that the basis for his knowledge seems reasonable. Red flags should go up if the basis of the knowledge is not firsthand but rather double or triple hearsay. In some instances, the publisher may demand to know who the source is and interrogate the source himself. Even if the publisher does all this, however, he should know that he may not be able to rely on the reliability of the source in court if he is not willing to reveal the source's identity so that the other side can challenge the source's reliability.

Finally, a publisher should be willing to retract a false statement if he learns of the falsehood after publication because the printing of a retraction will go a long way toward keeping down the damages awarded in the event the subject of the defamatory piece elects to sue anyway. Presumably, once a retraction is printed, the harm to the subject's reputation is mitigated.

Ideally, since both publishers and writers can be found guilty of libel, they should work together to ensure that published works treat subjects ethically and stay within the boundaries set by libel law. Fact-checking and other similar precautions may sometimes seem to be time-consuming annoyances, but they protect both writers and publishers and help ensure that the story is right the first time.

The Lyric Essay

Rod Stewart once sang, "Every picture tells a story don't it?"

True enough, but like pictures, some stories tend toward realism while others transform, adjust, and abstract the subject at hand. Enter the lyric essay.

Usually more ruminative than anecdotal, at times experimental and idiosyncratic, the lyric essay borrows as liberally from the poet's toolbox as it does from the techniques of prose narrative.

Deborah Tall and John D'Agata, writing in the *Seneca Review*, offer this definition: "Given its genre mingling, the lyric essay often accretes by fragments, taking shape mosaically—its import visible only when one stands back and sees it whole. The stories it tells may be no more than metaphors. Or, storyless, it may spiral in on itself, circling the core of a single image or idea, without climax, without a paraphrasable theme. The lyric essay stalks its subject like quarry but is never content to merely explain or confess. It elucidates through the dance of its own delving."

In other words, when compared with conventional memoir or narrative journalism, the lyric essay is a prose horse of an entirely different color. The story of a lyric essay has less to do with what happened, when it happened, or whether it was the result of some action than with the author's studying a thought, idea, or concept from numerous angles, turning it over and around, seeing what cognitive connections might arise. In this way the lyric essay is very much like the personal essay as defined by Phillip Lopate in his classic anthology *The Art of the Personal Essay.* Lopate writes, "The hallmark of the personal essay is its intimacy. The writer seems to be speaking directly into your ear, confiding everything from gossip to wisdom."

The word "essay" comes from the French word *essai,* meaning "trial" or "attempt." The lyric essay, taking that origin directly to heart, often meanders, with little, if any, resolution. What matters in this type of writing is the journey of the author's mind, the movement of idea and thought.

Brenda Miller and Suzanne Paola, in *Tell It Slant: Writing and Shaping Creative Nonfiction,* trace the lyric essay back to such writers as Seneca, Bacon, and Montaigne. Contemporary practitioners include Miller, Tall, D'Agata, Lia Purpura, and George W. S. Trow.

Another strong proponent of the lyric essay movement is author David Shields, who compares the lyric essay with Shakespeare's famous play about the indecisive Danish prince: "*Hamlet* is, more than anything else, Hamlet talking about a multitude of different topics. I find myself wanting to ditch the tired old plot altogether and just harness the voice, which is a processing machine, taking input and spitting out perspective—a lens, a distortion effect."

To put it another way, had Salvador Dali been a writer instead of a painter, he probably would have written lyric essays. In multicolored ink.

The Memoir Craze

"This is the age of memoir," observes William Zinsser in *Inventing the Truth: The Art and Craft of Memoir*. "Never have personal narratives gushed so profusely from the American soil as in the closing decade of the 20th century. Everyone has a story to tell, and everyone is telling it." Lorraine Adams, a columnist for the *Washington Post*, has dubbed this trend the rise of "the nobody memoir."

To trace the arc of memoir through the centuries, from St. Augustine to Mary Karr, would require a book-length manuscript. Memoirists have typically been heavy hitters: Johann Wolfgang von Goethe, Virginia Woolf, Henry David Thoreau, Walt Whitman, E. B. White, Gertrude Stein, Ulysses S. Grant, Mahatma Gandhi, Bill Clinton, Gore Vidal, George Orwell, Leon Trotsky, Benjamin Franklin, Mark Twain, Maya Angelou, Frederick Douglass, Black Elk, Helen Keller, Carl Jung, Jean-Paul Sartre, and on and on. But look beyond the list of notables, and you'll find a genre that practically guarantees a populist platform.

What critics overlook is that many notables would have remained nobodies if it weren't for their self-directed gazes. Moreover, the tradition of the nobody narrative is rich and stems from a reform impulse, a railing against the political by trotting forth the personal. Slave narratives, such as Harriet Jacobs's *Incidents in the Life of a Slave Girl*, were commissioned to highlight the inhumanities of slavery and sway the public with the specificity of the experiences related. Since the 1960s groups marginalized or overlooked by society have made their way to the center by the power of one person's personal story. In *I Know Why the Caged Bird Sings*, the young Maya Angelou begins to pee down her legs in church and knows she can't hold it because "it would probably run right back up to my head and my poor head would burst like a dropped watermelon, and all the brains and spit and tongue and eyes would roll all over the place." With this, we are running out the church door with her, and the release becomes metaphoric and multilayered, an almost joyful triumph over death, and no matter what our race, we can't help being tucked into the skin of a little girl growing up black in the South.

The nobodies of the world have no doubt been inspired to write by the recent successes of memoirs by average people. Literary timelines will mark the mid-1990s as the period of the genre's revival. Mary Karr's *The Liars' Club*, published in 1995, offered a story as dark and funny as any piece of fiction—except this stuff was real—and it sat on the *New York Times* best seller list for a year. In 1996, Frank McCourt, a high school teacher who had grown up poor in Ireland, published a memoir, *Angela's Ashes*, that went on to earn him a Pulitzer Prize.

When you look at our tendency these days to interface with technology rather than one another, perhaps the surprise is not that memoirs are flourishing but that anyone questions the trend. Neuropsychologists are discovering that the impulse for story is likely hard-wired into our brains. The less we talk to one another, the more our personal narratives—our confessions, our dark sides, our recitations of the things we do in secret—will seek other ways to emerge, finding voice in the genre of memory.

Metaphor

Metaphor, as everyone learns in elementary school, is the comparison of two unlike things, usually for the purpose of providing a new way to look at one, or maybe even both, of the things. To go a little beyond elementary school, the two "things" are technically called the tenor and the vehicle, the tenor being the main subject and the vehicle being the thing the comparison is drawn from. (For example, in Shakespeare's "Juliet is the sun," Juliet is the tenor, and the sun is the vehicle.)

The careful use of metaphor in writing can offer freshness and vitality to language. Using an extended metaphor can artfully lead readers to draw myriad comparisons between two subjects, without requiring the writer to draw the connections explicitly.

A striking use of extended, embedded metaphor occurs in Michael Oppenheimer's "Exposure," which examines the relationship between the young Michael and his father, Robert Oppenheimer, the physicist who headed the Manhattan Project. The younger Oppenheimer does not openly discuss his father's involvement with the creation of the atom bomb; instead, he focuses on a childhood incident, which taken alone is a subtle portrayal of a father-son relationship but when juxtaposed against Oppenheimer's professional accomplishments leads to a provocative reading of the man.

The only mention of the nuclear threat comes as prelude to the main scene of the essay. The author describes walking home, recalling a school lesson in which he was instructed to crawl into a culvert should America come under nuclear attack. "Do you think we'll be bombed?" Michael asks his sister. "No, but maybe in Korea," she responds.

Upon arriving home, the children are met by their father, who asks if they would like to help him butcher a steer. Michael agrees. His description of the event is meticulous, giving particular attention to his father's actions: "While he loaded the rifle, my dad told me, as he had the last time we butchered, about drawing two imaginary lines from the steer's ears to his eyes and then shooting the steer where the lines crossed. He said, 'That's where the most critical part of the brain is, and they're killed instantly without knowing what hit them.' The steer was looking at us, and I was glad he didn't know what was about to happen."

Michael's father takes aim and fires, but he has loaded the gun with the wrong ammunition and only wounds the steer's face. He leaves Michael in the pen with the anxious beast while he goes to find the proper ammunition. The story continues: "Finally my dad returned, and he took the rifle from me and put one shell in, raised the rifle to his shoulder, aimed, turning as the steer trotted, and then yelled loudly, 'Hey!' The steer stopped running, and we stood there waiting. Then the steer slowly turned his head toward us. His nose was inches from the dirt. His white face was splashed all over with blood, and he looked like he knew what was about to happen."

Michael Oppenheimer never explicitly comments on his

relationship with his father, nor does he expressly compare the humane death his father intends to give the steer with the intended effect of an atomic blast. The juxtaposition of the two scenes along with the knowledge of the father's identity, however, is more than sufficient to create a chain of comparisons. The unfortunate steer is like the victims of nuclear devastation in that it dies more horribly than the killer intends. The steer is also like all people who know the psychic distress of living in the nuclear age; it, like humans, bears the immeasurable burden of knowledge. The son's discovery that his father is fallible is like the nation's discovery that its scientists and statesmen are fallible, that even though the nation possesses the ultimate weapon, its people are more vulnerable than ever before.

All these connections are driven by the dual identity of Robert Oppenheimer; the genius physicist, director of the Manhattan Project, is also a rural farmer butchering his livestock. His shortcomings necessarily infiltrate both facets of his character. Errors in his procedure for killing a steer, his misloading of the gun and his lack of insight into the experience of the steer, bespeak fallibility and ignorance that extend to his participation in the Manhattan Project.

In fiction, the full effect of metaphor can sometimes be undercut by the context-driven assumption that "it's just a story." A metaphor is clearly an author's construction, inserted to manipulate readers subtly. Of course, the use of metaphor is no less a writerly conceit in creative nonfiction, but because the comparison is based in fact, it can carry more weight. Careful recording and thoughtful reflection can capture such real-life identities and metaphors. In cultivating an awareness for these, creative nonfiction writers claim an immensely powerful tool.

Montage Writing

Montage writing, also called segmented, snapshot, or collage writing, is immediately recognizable on the page: Sections of writing, often very short, are separated one from the next by asterisks or white space. Montage is also immediately recognizable in the reading; there is a sense that a camera shutter closes and opens, closes and opens as we move from segment to segment. The effect is familiar; films are almost always montaged editings of separate "moments." We move through films with that steady closing out of one scene and the unannounced opening of the next, fluidly and confidently. We expect this constantly shifting "eye" in a film. In the same way, as readers of montaged essays, we make the shift intuitively from segment to segment. A montaged essay draws the reader and writer together in an interpretive duet.

*

The asterisk signals a shift. The lens shutter closes and snaps open in a new and mostly unconnected realm. A discontinuity of images, scenes, and observations creates a dialogue in space and time, asking the reader to close and open the eyes,

close and open the eyes, at each opening discovering another
component of a suggested truth. The segments of a montaged
essay accrue to new and larger ideas that might weight a continuous narrative into opacity. In each new opening of the lens
shutter, the reader is invited anew, moment to moment, to
imagine the scaffolding, the architecture of the whole.

*

Perhaps the montage is a chronicle, as in Sherman Alexie's
"Captivity," which is numbered one to fourteen:

13

All we can depend on are the slow-motion replays
of our lives. Frame 1: Lester reaches for the next beer.
Frame 2: He pulls it to his face by memory, drinks it
like a 20th-century vision. Frame 3: He tells a joke,
sings another song: *Well, they sent me off to boarding
school and made me learn the white man's rules.*

*

Each segment is a juxtaposition of narrative or image or
reflection. What is left out is as important as what is said; the
white field in between creates tension, expectation, just as the
stanzas of a poem signal a shift forward, to the side, back. A
montaged essay excludes much more than it writes.

*

Perhaps the montaged essay is a list, like this, each segment a shift

in time

In his memoir *Running in the Family*, Michael Ondaatje travels to India, moving backward and forward through family memory. He opens the first segment by telling us, "What began it all was the bright bone of a dream I could hardly hold onto." Later he moves backward, opening a short segment with this: "The early twenties had been a busy and expensive time for my grandparents." He gets confused as he walks back into his family story and opens a segment protesting, "Wait a minute, wait a minute! When did all this happen, I'm trying to get it straight. . . ."

in interior time

Primo Levi, in *Survival in Auschwitz*, moves from memory to memory steadily, inexorably, suggesting the unspeakable. He opens one segment, "And for the first time since I entered the camp the reveille catches me in a deep sleep and its ringing is a return from nothingness." Another: "We fought with all our strength to prevent the arrival of winter." Then: "We have a great many things to learn, but we have learned many already." Just before rescue: "We lay in a world of death and phantoms. The last trace of civilization has vanished around and inside us."

in place

John McPhee, in "The Search for Marvin Gardens," moves between a Monopoly game board and the parallel world of streets and social history. Atlantic City becomes a dream landscape. We play the game with him: "Go. Roll the dice—a six and a two." Then: "The dogs are moving (some are limping) through ruins, rubble, fire damage, open garbage," and "Visiting hours are daily, eleven to two . . . Immediate Family Only Allowed in Jail."

from image to reflection

Annie Dillard invites us to witness an eclipse, leaping from image to reflection, physics to metaphysics: "It began with no ado." Later: "The second before the sun went out we saw a wall of shadow come speeding at us. We no sooner saw it than it was upon us, like thunder. . . . It slammed the hill and knocked us out." Then her leap: "The world which lay under darkness and stillness following the closing of the lid was not the world we know."

and from image to metaphor

Albert Goldbarth, in "Delft," studies fleas as he shifts between Vermeer's vision of Delft and Antoni van Leeuwenhoek's vision through the lens of the first microscope: Goldbarth opens, "He cometh unto his kingdom now. . . . Call him Leeuwenhoek." Later: "If we enter Delft through his [Vermeer's] *View of Delft* . . ." and finally, "This story's this simple: the tiniest units that introduce love, conduct huge suffering."

*

The montaged essay is an intuitive gesture, for writer and for reader. The shutter clicks, and the film moves on. Click, and we are caught by the memory of our father's hands. Click, and those hands belong to a young man at boot camp. Click, and the light of an early-winter snowfall carries us to the sadness of a quiet house many years ago. Click, and our own hands weave the story. What we include is vital. Each segment is a small universe, suggestive, seductive, elliptical. What we choose not to say is vital; the empty space on the page adds its voice to the idea, which is perhaps larger, less definable, less confined than it might be if it moved in a more dialectical way through the essay. There are no transitions, a wonderful freedom, and also a warning to the writer: There is no road map. Beware! Your reader may wander off your path. The writer must ask: Where am I going? In the end, exacting strategies for cohesion and movement provide the architecture, an invitation to your reader to trust you.

*

Or perhaps the shift is
               from the now to the backstory
   or
               between points of view
   or
               from prayer to prayer

*

Themes emerge unannounced to the writer, surprising and mysterious. We make choices: Now I shall write this segment. Not this. Yes, this. We do not know the reasons yet. But suddenly water flows through every segment. Light illuminates.

Loss, or reclaimed belief, or the perpetual need to be loved. History and beauty and dreams and small spoken words are, for the moment, all there is. We focus attention. The intensity of the moment concedes to the next, and the next, those spaces in between offering respite, time enough for the reader to imagine, to splice together the whole. The shutter clicks, and the reader is ready.

The Narrative Impulse

It's been ten years since James Atlas declared ours "the age of the literary memoir" in the *New York Times*, and the public's appetite for true tales of the self, imaginatively told, seems boundless. The demand for fiction continues to fizzle, while first-time memoirists build the kind of buzz that once befitted big-name novelists. Some claim it's a fad, a filling of the literary troughs with sentimental slop. Yet recent research regarding the brain would suggest that narratives of self—both the telling (writing) and the hearing (reading)—stem from impulses basic to our being.

We've learned that the mind is malleable, that the brain's neural pathways constantly rewire themselves to order sensory input, creating connections among disparate facts and ultimately spinning explanations about the self in the world. In essence, the mind "is telling itself a story," notes David Suzuki in *The Sacred Balance: Rediscovering Our Place in Nature*. He argues that this knack for narrative enabled our ancestors to recognize, understand, and remember the meaning of patterns in nature, such as the migrations of animals, the sequencing of the seasons, and the duration of night and day.

These observations become memories, and the meanings

they form transcend what we need to survive physically; they form a dynamic interplay with our emotions and thoughts that is essential to our psychological survival in a complex society. Not all our memories teem at the surface of our conscious thoughts, that is sure, unless we actively set about recollecting them. But taken together, our memories and perceptions form an autobiographical self, a set of personal myths and stories that give our lives meaning. In fact, people with certain brain impairments, such as occurs in Alzheimer's patients, have lost this ability to narrate their lives and develop a sort of existential bewilderment, a loss of personhood known as dysnarrativia.

We are not content to tell our stories to ourselves; we feel moved, even inspired to tell our stories to others. The storytelling urge begins early in life, notes Alice Weaver Flaherty in *The Midnight Disease: The Drive to Write, Writer's Block, and the Creative Brain.* She observes that children "compulsively narrate their experiences and desires," as anyone who has been subjected to a three-year-old's running commentary can attest. The act of autobiography forms in our frontal cortices, while the will to write likely lies in the limbic system, one of the oldest parts of the brain, governing not only basic desires for food and sex but social bonding, learning, and memories. We are the most vocal of the primates, and sharing the intimate details of our lives has many functions: The act makes us feel connected to others, alleviates stress, and makes us healthier. Writing about emotionally laden events increases our T-cell growth and antibody response, lowers our heart rate, helps us lose weight, improves sleep, elevates our mood, and can even reduce pain.

Given the importance of sharing stories, we should not

be surprised that the age of literary memoir has flourished in an age of disconnection. We belong to fewer civic groups, spend less time with friends and family, and log a month more hours at work than we did in the 1960s, outstripping even the work-fanatic Japanese. Even picnics per capita declined 60 percent between 1975 to 1999, Robert D. Putnam notes in *Bowling Alone: The Collapse and Revival of American Community*. Technology has sped up our lives and increased our isolation. We tend to sojourn solely in the company of a computer, although high Internet usage corresponds with feelings of loneliness. We visit an automatic teller instead of a live one, run our purchases over do-it-yourself scanners at the grocery store, and secure our privacy in public with an armament of personal electronic devices. We watch reality television shows to supplement a meager ration of interpersonal contact. Our voices and our stories become hidden in the steady babble of the information age.

Despite our isolation, we are drawn to story, and the more emotional the tale, the deeper the salient information lodges in our memories. We learn from personal revelations, war stories, family legends, urban myths, campfire tales, true confessions, and gossip around the water cooler. James Wolcott, contributing editor for *Vanity Fair*, has sniggered at memoir for pandering to the voyeuristic and aspiring toward the lofty realm of redemption, yet living a life filled with suffering is precisely the existential itch that the genre scratches. The various subcategories within memoir mark the passages through being human: childhood, adolescence, love, sex, child rearing, illness, dissolution, aging, war, imprisonment, enslavement, abuse, addiction, healing, journeys, spirituality, the unknown, and death itself. The telling of tales does more than entertain.

It transmits important information between generations, making important events of the past relevant. A genre that appears to be narcissistic is, in truth, outward-directed, actually eclipsing the experience of the individual and speaking to society. The memoir multiplied creates a million little connections, threading an otherwise fragmented postmodern world with the narrative of human meaning.

Navel-gazing

Danny Bonaduce, poster boy for former child stars gone wild, stares straight into the camera. "My life is a train wreck," he says. "You're welcome to watch."

This was the promo for *Breaking Bonaduce*, a controversial reality series starring the steroid-pumped but still freckly Bonaduce, his sighing wife, Gretchen, and their VH1-appointed therapist, Dr. Garry.

Bonaduce has always made good television. Years ago he was cute little Danny Partridge, the youngest member of the 1970s Partridge Family and the one who most resembled a Cabbage Patch doll. Now, all grown up and without Shirley Jones to turn to for motherly advice, Bonaduce is a mess. His marriage is on the fritz. He's tried to commit suicide. He has a multitude of addictions, including sex and drugs and porn. And he's likely violent. Remember the incident years ago when he beat up a transvestite and it made the news? VH1 certainly did. Can anyone say Nielsen ratings?

The show was, predictably, a hit for VH1, which has since become king of the celebrity reality TV circus. At the end of the first season of *Breaking Bonaduce*, viewers who'd tuned in to watch Danny rant into his cell phone, threaten Dr. Garry, threaten to slit his own wrists, actually slit his wrists and then explain his bandages to his young daughter were rewarded with—what exactly?

The understanding that Danny Bonaduce's life is, well, a mess.

The revelation that this often happens to former child stars.

The knowledge that this is, perhaps, sad.

End of story.

If you think Bonaduce and those like him are confined to television, that most maligned pop culture medium, just check out the memoir/biography/self-help section of your local megabookstore. You might notice some similarities.

Here's a title that, according to a certain publishing/marketing trend, would get powerful talk show hosts' panties in a twist: *A Heartbreaking Work of Staggering Ex-Crackhead Cross-Dressing Male One-Legged Club-Footed Prostitute Whose Adulterous Midget Heroin-Addicted Mama Fed Him Rancid Dog Food through a Straw Then Sold Him to the CIA for One Mottled Banana and a Pack of Kool Menthols: A True Story.*

Apologies to Dave Eggers, who is, as he notes in his own title, most likely a genius. But back to the point.

Memoirs and personal essay collections are everywhere these days, and despite what some critics say, this is not a bad thing. There are so many wonderful, human, funny, powerful, and true stories out there. (Try Ann Patchett's *Truth & Beauty*, a sad and inspiring story of friendship; Greg Bottoms's *Angelhead*, a haunting story about what it's like to grow up in a family one of whose members is mentally ill; Kathy Dobie's incisive *The Only Girl in the Car*, a story about a girl coming of age in a brutal small town.) But there is also a trend toward the other side of memoir, the Bonaduce side, the side that says, "My pain is greater than anyone else's pain." The side that says, "Look at me. I'm so crazy. No one has ever been this crazy, and no one will be this crazy ever again." The side that says, "Look at me. Look at *me*."

Come on.

Books should not be the equivalent of reality TV. Memoir writing—despite what William Grimes said in a critique for the *New York Times*, "We All Have a Life. Must We All Write About It?"—is not about navel-gazing.

(The phrase, by the way, is a contemporary take on ompha-loskepsis, the practice whereby contemplative folks like monks and mystics and Grateful Dead enthusiasts gaze for days at their own navels, hoping to find, tucked in the intricate maze of their own centers, the keys to divine enlightenment and/or their cars.)

Memoir writing is not about self-obsession, even though the subject is invariably the experience of one life.

Good memoirs should do what all good art aspires to do. They should show us ourselves. This is arguably the distinc-tion between good and bad memoir writing. Bad memoirs often offer readers the book equivalent of reality TV. They pro-vide voyeuristic pleasure, the chance to peek into the under-wear drawer of a writer who's done more crack, made more kissy-face with his/her father/mother, punched out more cops, drunk more booze, and racked up more hours in rehab and on therapists' couches than anyone else. Ever.

Sure, some of these memoirs are more titillating than oth-ers. Then again, some navels contain fluffier or dirtier or more interesting belly lint than others. Recently a man in Canada reported that after a camping trip and a week without a shower, he looked down to find a sapling had sprouted smack in the center of his navel. He took pictures and posted them on the Internet.

Well then.

The point is that bad memoir writing, like bad television, involves navel-gazing and nothing more. The writer is so obsessed with him/herself that there is no concern for how that self fits into the big picture. And no matter how sensational or how boring the life of the bad memoir writer may be, the reader comes away with the same thing.

Wow.

Gee.

Isn't that something?

What kind of sapling was it anyway?

Is that so?

Wow.

A good memoir does more than that. A good memoir offers readers a human connection. A good memoir writer uses life experience, not to go more deeply into the self but to reach out to others. A good memoirist makes connections. A good memoirist's primary goal is to show us something true about ourselves, about what it means to be human.

"I am vast," Walt Whitman wrote. "I contain multitudes."

We all contain multitudes. We all contain universal truths.

"We're born, we live a little while, we die." E. B. White's Charlotte, the spider, spelled it out for us.

We each come to this understanding through a life filled with individual experiences. Those individual experiences are what make up a memoirist's subject. Some of those experiences are worth writing about; others aren't. Some people are born writers; others aren't. These aren't things that can or should be chosen or invented simply to fit a marketing niche. In a line meant as advice for young writers who romanticize suffering as a means to a creative life, the poet Carolyn Forche wrote: "Twenty-year-old poet / Hikmet did not choose to be Hikmet."

Nâzim Hikmet. The great Turkish poet who wrote some of his most important poems on prison toilet paper. Hikmet. A man who spent more than twenty-six of his sixty-one years either in solitary confinement or in exile. Hikmet, the author of the great epic *Human Landscapes* as well as many intimate narrative poems that reflect on everything from his experiences in prison to, a month before his death, a meditation on what it means to be alive:

> *I mean you must take living so seriously*
> *that even at seventy, for example, you will plant*
> *olives—*

Those olives, Hikmet said, would be an act of defiance. Human beings, he said, fear death, but we don't believe it will come for us.

Hikmet did not choose to be Hikmet.

Hikmet didn't play to cameras or to a publishing market. He didn't invent. He didn't overdramatize. He simply played the hand he had been dealt. He wrote from his own experience, his own center. He didn't do this because he was obsessed with the labyrinth of his own suffering or his own navel. He did not write inward, though he had every excuse to do so. Instead he wrote outward. While in prison, he wrote poems addressed in the second person, though he may not have believed that anyone else would ever read them. He wrote poems to others who were imprisoned, either literally or figuratively. He offered advice on how to survive.

To survive, Hikmet said, we all must be connected to the world and not separate from it. We must be caught up in, and not disengaged from, what he called "the flurry of the world."

Bonaduce is, for ratings' sake, a flurry of his own making. He is separate from the rest of us. As it's presented by VH1, his life is a spectacle, something to watch, not something to mirror our own. That's what separates television and navel-gazing from real art. Individual human experience is valuable—in writing and elsewhere—only when it moves through, then transcends the self and connects to what's human in us all.

Point of View

OBI-WAN: So what I told you was TRUE . . . from a certain point
of view.

LUKE: A certain point of view?

OBI-WAN: Luke, you're going to find that many of the truths we
cling to . . . depend greatly on our own points of view.

—*Star Wars: Episode VI—Return of the Jedi*

I think that I have discovered a possible form for these notes.
That is, to make them include the present—at least enough of
the present to serve as a platform to stand upon. It would be
interesting to make the two people—I now, I then—come out in
contrast. And further, this past is much affected by the present
moment. What I write today I should not write in a year's time.

—Virginia Woolf, "A Sketch of the Past"

In creative nonfiction, especially in personal narratives, we
can easily begin to feel imprisoned by the bars of "I, I, I" that
tend to pepper our prose. Our points of view can feel limited,
isolated, or small. But if, as Virginia Woolf suggests, we perch
on a platform for viewing the past, why not invite a multiplicity
of spectators to join us there? The variables of point of view in
creative nonfiction can be just as numerous and just as effective as those used in fiction and poetry, perhaps even more so

since the point (or points) of view in which we choose to tell our stories could be the point of the story as well. As the wise Obi-Wan so succinctly tells us, truth is not a fixed adage but a concept that shifts under our gaze, multifaceted, determined by whatever self or persona happens to be in charge at the moment.

In fact, when we think of the term "point of view" in all its implications, we can see that it's really an essential aspect of creative nonfiction's groundwork. "Try to see it from *my* point of view," we often say in heated conversation, or "It's *my* point of view," when we're trying to put forth an argument or an opinion. But these phrases often make it seem as though a point of view were a fixed thing, immutable, easily ascertained. The joy of writing and reading creative nonfiction can be precisely that we come to have a multidimensional apprehension of the "truth" of experience. Sometimes this approach means that we will employ literal point of view digressions, such as second or third person, but we might consider variables of the I-narrator as different points of view as well.

Often we assume that if we speak in an I-voice, it is always the same I. But this I is shaped by time, by experience, and by mood. There's the I with a sense of humor about the whole thing, the I who is still puzzled, the I who has wisdom to impart, the I who has an ax to grind. There is also what we might call the Lyric I: the I who is silent; the I who speaks through fragmentation, through pure observation, through white space, the I who disappears into the gaps, eclipsed by language and metaphor.

We can also think of point of view as donning a pair of binoculars. How far can we see across time and space? Tense and time are just as much a part of point of view as the use of first, second, or third person. When we speak from a child's point of view in the present tense, it is obviously not the child writing the prose, but us imagining ourselves into her point of view for a while, and the present tense lends itself to the immediacy of such childlike encounters. And when we look back on that child from the adult point of view, we are pretending to be a wiser adult, but it's still a mere persona, or point of view, we're assuming and trying to make credible. When we imagine a time before we were born—imagining the points of view of our parents or grandparents, say—we are assuming a high-powered pair of binoculars. Here we are stretching the boundaries of creative nonfiction but still staying in that realm since we give clues that this is not a literal truth but an imaginative one. We are exercising our facilities of empathy.

Bernard Cooper, in *Truth Serum*, often uses the future tense, looking ahead beyond the moment he's describing, using key phrases such as "I don't yet know that . . ." or "I can't know it at the time, but. . . ." These kinds of phrases automatically elicit a complex sense of point of view: The narrator is consciously positioned in a place where he knows both the past and the future; therefore, the point of view is not necessarily the author's but that of a persona he has created to afford the best view of both.

So these issues of point of view really point to one of the most fundamental skills in creative nonfiction, to writing not as the "author" but from a constructed persona, even if that persona is taking on the "I" to tell the story. That persona is formed by time, mood, and distance from the events that are being narrated. And if we decide to foreground the artifice of this construction by using more stylized points of view, such as second and third person, we create even more of a relationship between the narrator and the narrated, a high awareness that we are engaged in the reconstruction of experience and not pretending to be mere transcribers of that experience.

Some Variables You (or I/One/We/She/He/They) Might Consider When Thinking About Point of View in Creative Nonfiction

The "I" point of view (first person, singular and/or plural: How far can "I" see?)

- First person, present, childlike.
- First person, present, adult.
- First person, past, looking back (into the distance or just to yesterday).
- First person, future (looking ahead).
- First person, moody: variables of the "I" that determine voice—funny, rueful, nostalgic, earnest, sad, etc.
- The Lyric I: speaking through silence, poetic devices, or other forms/voices (for example, use of the fragmented braided essay form or the collage essay, where white space implies silence and meaning is created through oblique connections of images and metaphors rather than through a straightforward narrative story).
- The "I" who is "we" or "one" (from Virginia Woolf's "Street Haunting": "No one perhaps has ever felt passionately toward a lead pencil. But there are circumstances in which it can become supremely desirable to possess one; moments when we are set upon having an object, an excuse for walking

half across London between tea and dinner. . . . The hour should be the evening and the season winter . . .").

The "you" point of view (second person, singular and/or plural)

- The commanding "you" (as in how to pieces): the "you" that is kind of the "I" but could also be "You" (from Brenda Miller's "How to Meditate": "On arrival, huddle in the Volkswagen with your friends and eat all the chocolate in the car. Chocolate chips, old KitKats, the tag end of a Hershey's bar—do not discriminate.").
- The "you" who is definitely the "I": talking to yourself, about yourself, by way of talking to the reader (from Nick Flynn's *Another Bullshit Night in Suck City*: "If you had been raised in a village 200 years ago, somewhere in Eastern Europe, say, or even on the coast of Massachusetts, and your father was a drunk, or a little off, or both, then everyone in the village, those you grew up with and those who knew you only from a distance, they would all know that the town drunk or the village idiot was your father. . . . They would look into your eyes to see if they were his eyes, they would notice if you were to stumble slightly as you stepped into a shop, they would remember that your father, too, had started with promise, like you").
- The "you" who is definitely "you": direct address to another character (implies an "I" is speaking)

(from Abigail Thomas's *Safekeeping*: "Before I met
you I played my music on a child's Victrola. . . .
I am remembering this time just before I knew
you, and then I knew you, and then you died. It
makes the parentheses within which I lived most
of my life. Not knowing you, knowing you, and
then you died").
- The "you" who is all of us: "You do this. You do
that. . . ."

**The "she/he/they" point of view (third person, omniscient
or another character's perspective altogether)**
- The "she" that is "I": speaking of the self in the
third person (from *Safekeeping*: "A middle-aged
teacher is walking down Broadway in her big white
sneakers and her yellow socks, her too long skirt
(stained where three drops of hair-tinting stuff fell
on it); she is wearing her daughter's jacket, a new
red velvet scarf and her two haircuts, both bad,
and she is thinking about desire . . .").
- The "she" that is "she" told by an "I": describing
events you can't really know about, but maintaining a subtle "I" (from Paisley Rekdal's *The Night My
Mother Met Bruce Lee*: "Age 16, my mother loads
up red tubs of noodles, teacups chipped and white-
gray as teeth, rice clumps that glue themselves to
the plastic tub sides or dissolve and turn papery in
the weak tea sloshing around the bottom").
- The "he" that is really "he": inhabiting someone
else's point of view entirely (from *Another Bullshit
Night in Suck City*: "My father lifts the receiver in

the night, speaks into it, asks *Where's the money?*
Asks *Why can't I sleep?* Asks *Who left me outside?*
The phone rings on a desk when he lifts it, the
desk somewhere in Texas, someone is always
supposed to be at that desk but no one ever is,
not at night. A machine speaks while my father
tries to speak, it doesn't listen, it only speaks, my
father's face reflected dimly on the screen").

All these variables are artistic constructions, but if a particular technique is used too self-consciously, it may feel shallow,
like a gimmick. There must be some deeper reason to shift
point of view, and ideally the right point of view will find its way
to the writer, not the other way around. For instance, if we need
physical distance from the self in order to speak about the self
truthfully, then the third person point of view will enhance that
distance and help bolster the meaning of the essay. If we feel we
are writing a universal experience, not just a private one, the
second person point of view may come in handy. Point of view is
innately tied to voice, and a strong, well-executed point of view
will also lead to a strong voice, one that will be clearly heard
above the mayhem of the world.

Psychoanalyzing Characters

In his nonfiction best seller *The Devil in the White City,* Erik Larson delves deeply and convincingly into the mind of the serial killer H. H. Holmes. In fact, making use of newspaper accounts, trial transcripts, and other source material, he goes so far as to refute aspects of Holmes's autobiography, written in prison before his execution. Larson challenges many of the killer's descriptions of his feelings and motivations, inserting his own analysis of Holmes's state of mind.

In his notes at book's end, Larson makes a pretty compelling case for his justification in doing this. But this technique does raise a fascinating question for creative nonfiction writers. What are the dangers of such "psychoanalyzing" when depicting the inner workings of a real person's mind? Is this not practicing therapy without a license?

It's a charge frequently leveled at nonfiction writers, especially those like Bob Woodward and Doris Kearns Goodwin, who specialize in "re-creating" the thoughts and feelings of historical figures. In the past two decades, biographers of famous individuals have been even more liberal—some might say audacious—in their attempts at psychoanalytic interpretation of their subjects. Hence we've seen speculation that Abraham Lincoln and Eleanor Roosevelt were gay, famed child psychologist Bruno Bettelheim was a pathological liar, and Adolf Hitler was sexually abused.

The point is, today's nonfiction writers delve more intimately than ever into the lives and subjective experiences of the real people they depict. While this approach has always been a crucial component of the fiction writer's art, there's a specific danger involved when the people depicted actually exist—namely, that much of the authority behind the nonfiction writer's voice (and opinion) derives from the reader's belief that what's being described is "true."

Does this mean there are never circumstances when the thoughts, feelings, and motivations of people you're writing about can't be creatively imagined? Not necessarily. Narrative requires that people *do* things, and in life as well as in fiction, people do things for reasons, even if those reasons make sense only to them. To be deprived of the opportunity to extrapolate what these reasons might be is to sacrifice much of what makes reading about people interesting and compelling in the first place.

The danger emerges when the nonfiction writer assumes a false sense of objective distance from the inner world of the person being depicted. Whether reading the person's journal, scouring contemporary accounts of the person's actions, or talking with family members and intimate friends about the subject's personality and habits, the writer must remember that he or she *also* brings something to the table, a wealth of personal experiences, prejudices, and intentions of his or her own.

For example, if you're interviewing someone about the details of his failed marriage, your own relationship experiences create a filter through which you see, hear, and draw conclusions about what the subject is saying.

In other words, whether doing research about events that happened before you were born, or as a result of spending the past two weeks living in almost continual contact with your subject, you're bringing so much of your own history and expectations and beliefs into the mix that it's presumptuous to assume you're "seeing" things in a completely objective way.

(To take an extreme example, it could be argued that Richard Pollack's biography of Bruno Bettelheim, mentioned above, is undeniably influenced by the fact that Pollack's brother was a patient who died under suspicious circumstances while in Bettelheim's care.)

Is there a way for nonfiction writers to explore the possible feelings and motives of their characters that makes narrative sense, is psychologically astute and persuasive, yet still respects the limitations of what the writer can truly know? The answer is yes, if it's done with skill and a real awareness of these limitations.

Among recent examples, perhaps the best is Sebastian Junger's *The Perfect Storm*. Without much real information about the ship captain's decision-making process, or the manner in which the ship was lost, or even a clue to *one single event* that actually transpired during the fishing trip, Junger managed to convey his understanding of the rigors of swordfishing as well as the various navigational choices available to the crew as the storm approached. He also presented a moving and vivid depiction of what the experience of drowning might feel like. This all was accomplished by his clearly stating that what he was describing was based on conjecture, the experiences of other fishermen he'd interviewed, and the utilization of his own imagination.

This presentation invites the reader to go on a journey into Junger's created impression of what might have happened. What results has the ring of truth, rather than the solidity of fact, and is perhaps the more powerful because of it.

In other words, rather than practice therapy without a license, the task for the creative nonfiction writer becomes, as always, about simply practicing the art of good writing.

Quotation Marks

Quotation marks signal to readers that these are a person's exact words. But what can nonfiction writers do when they're not sure they have before them a speaker's exact words?

It's hardly a secret that some writers, particularly when writing memoirs, accounts of past events they weren't keeping records of, do the best they can at re-creating dialogue and place those re-creations within quotation marks. Readers make allowances for this, understanding, as Daniel Nester put it in "Notes on Frey," that dialogue in memoir is "an emblematic device to remind us that This Important Discussion took place." (Nester also points out that whatever sins of falsification James Frey might have committed, he chose not to use quotation marks for dialogue in *A Million Little Pieces*.)

Not all writers (or readers, for that matter) are satisfied with this solution, however, and new conventions rise to meet the challenges of nonfiction. That's part of the excitement of the creative nonfiction form. One of the most useful innovations may be dialogue *without* quotation marks. Frank McCourt used this approach in *Angela's Ashes*, and Sebastian Junger in *The Perfect Storm*.

Leaving out the quotation marks can, paradoxically, signal levels of certainty. When writing *Schindler's List*, his tale of Holocaust rescue, Thomas Keneally faced a problem. For many of the World War II scenes he wished to reconstruct, he had multiple witnesses confirming the speakers' precise words. Few witnesses of other key scenes survived, however, or if they did, the distance in time caused Keneally to be less sure of the accuracy of the recalled words. For these moments he turned to dialogue sans quotation marks. In the helpful author note that launches *Schindler's List*, he explains: "It has sometimes been necessary to make reasonable constructs of conversations of which Oskar [Schindler] and others have left only the briefest record."

Many scenes in Keneally's volume unfold with dialogue *in* quotation marks. Others employ dialogue *without* the marks, and on occasion, the scrupulous writer even mixes the two. For example, to re-create one of Schindler's earliest and most daring acts to pluck Jews from Hitler's death trains, Keneally pens this scene:

> But Schindler was a philosophic innocent. He knew the people he knew. He knew the name of Bankier. *"Bankier! Bankier!"* he continued to call.
>
> He was intercepted by a young SS *Oberscharführer*, an expert railroad shipper from Lublin. He asked for Schindler's pass. Oskar could see in the man's left hand an enormous list—pages of names.
>
> My workers, said Schindler. Essential industrial workers. My office manager. It's idiocy. I have Armaments Inspectorate contracts, and here you are taking the workers I need to fulfill them.
>
> You can't have them back, said the young man.

> They're on the list. . . . The SS NCO knew from experience that the list conferred an equal destination on all its members.

Odd as it first might seem, the lack of quotation marks in this passage actually creates an extraordinary effect. It acknowledges Keneally's uncertainty of the precise words the men exchanged, yet at the same time the words' liberation from quote marks, with their implied anchor to a specific time, moves the scene toward the timeless and elemental. Keneally's whole story seems encapsuled in this tiny tableau. Another curious phenomenon occurs: After a while readers hardly notice whether the dialogue is in or out of quotation marks, so caught up are they in the drama. Nevertheless, the distinction is there for the scrupulous reader or thinker.

Reconstruction of Events

Our memories function as though we have an internal, private documentary film about our entire lives; only it's been formatted to the wrong video software, and it scrambles across different files on several bad disks. We grab what scenes and sound bites we can, the ones that are still whole, wait to see what surfaces from the depths on its own and then drag the river for the rest, piecing the fragments together. When writing from memory, you reconstruct as best as you can, and you give a nod or two to the flaws, the gaps in your recollection.

Sometimes there are records to help fill in these gaps, but even they may not be perfect sources of information. In *Girl, Interrupted*, her memoir of being institutionalized for two years in the late sixties, Susanna Kaysen writes, "I was wrong," about her recollection of her admittance. She remembered talking for twenty minutes with the doctor who committed her, though his admission note stated that he had interviewed her for more than three hours. "Both of us can't be right," Kaysen reasons, initially conceding, allowing the reader to believe that she is the one who must have misremembered the events. After all, the doctor's official report said he had taken three hours to determine her mental condition. However, the author then backs up her memory by introducing the times printed on her admittance documents, records that make it clear that while her doctor may have taken more than twenty minutes to diagnose her, it was impossible for him to have interviewed her for three hours. The reader has to entertain the possibility that Kaysen's memory of the event is the one that is accurate. Either way, her careful examination of the deviating accounts makes the reader wonder: What other mistakes might Kaysen's doctors have made?

Similarly, the details and dialogue we forget from our own lives can tell us a great deal about when and where to dive into our memories and begin reconstructing events. Memoirist and poet Mary Karr notes, "Sometimes to forget an event may be the most radiantly true way of representing it." On occasion, it is the scenes from our lives where the details and dialogues are the fuzziest that we should question and attempt to piece together, even if our memories are not perfect. Karr also reminds us to give credit to our audiences: "Readers understand, of course, that no one lives with a Handycam strapped to her head for research purposes."

It surprises many new nonfiction writers that they have to do research or reconnaissance on their own experiences. But frequently we do need to ask the other people involved, check documents, and visit and revisit our memories of events. We will probably not get it right the first time. We are constructing the movie script of our own existence from the cutting room floor. We will have to go back several times and question our scenes to see if they accurately render the events, the people involved, and their impact. The research we devote to looking for fragments within our own minds should be conducted with the same attention that we would devote to any other form of documented scenes. We should cull through the ashes a few times and, when possible, compare our memories with exterior sources.

Ultimately, what we have witnessed is ours to render, and our responsibility lies in rendering as accurately as possible the truth of the scenes as we remember them. We have a responsibility to convey scenes from our own lives with stunning visual and visceral detail so that our readers may have access to an existence beyond their own.

Reflection

In creative nonfiction, a writer may philosophize and add insight, telling a reader what the scenes and stories being so vividly chronicled and re-created mean both to the writer and to the world. This reflection is not mandated; scenes often speak for themselves. But in creative nonfiction a writer may step away from a narrative for a short time to ponder the meaning of a scene or to help readers understand the essence of the story being told.

John Edgar Wideman's essay "Looking at Emmett Till" tells the story of Till's murder—he was kidnapped by a group of angry white men in 1955 in Mississippi—and describes the impact of the event on Wideman's life. We learn in the essay that as a teenager in Pittsburgh, Wideman, who was the same age as Till, saw photographs of Till's body in *Jet*. The photographs and the murder have haunted him ever since, and even as an adult, he tells us, he periodically experiences shockingly vivid and frightening dreams in which he is being chased by a monster whose face he "can't bear to look upon," a face he has come to believe is Till's.

Midway through the essay, Wideman postulates that Till's murder "was an attempt to slay an entire generation. Push us backward to the bad old days when our lives seemed not to belong to us. When white power and racism seemed unchallengeable forces of nature, when inferiority and subserviency appeared to be our birthright, when black lives seemed cheap and expendable, when the grossest insults to pride and person, up to and including murder, had to be endured."

Here Wideman pauses to reflect, to add context and meaning, and to share his ideas about the symbolic impact of Till's assassination. He adds information and connects Till to the present-day murder of James Byrd in Texas, which, he says, reminds us "that the bad old days are never farther away than the thickness of skin, skin some people still claim the prerogative to burn or cut or shoot full of holes if it is dark skin."

Reflection relates to focus; a writer must stay on point. And reflection is not merely an opportunity for writers to editorialize. It is not exactly the writer's opinion the reader is seeking; rather, the reader wants to be able to understand and appreciate the ramifications of the narrative and the information embedded in it. If the writer can then help readers think more about the substance of the story, thereby making it more universal, reflection will enrich the reading experience.

The Roots of Memoir

A sixteen-year-old boy, lousy with lust and a certain lassitude, falls in with a fast crowd and one evening purloins the pears from a tree near his family's vineyard. He and his gang aren't particularly hungry; they sample a few and throw the rest to the hogs. That they've done something forbidden makes the thievery thrilling. "It was foul, and I loved it," the narrator recalls of the lark. "I loved my own undoing."

At a juncture when memoir is being criticized for its confessional aspects, for falling into the realm of the therapeutic, the narcissistic, and the lurid, for lapsing into so much navel-gazing, it's worth looking at the genre's antecedents. Augustine's recollection of stealing pears may seem like tame stuff to modern readers, but in A.D. 397, when the aptly named *Confessions* was released, his sinful life and the internal spiritual struggle he revealed created both a stir and a genre.

Similarly, had Jean-Jacques Rousseau written his memoir (also titled *Confessions*) today instead of in 1792, one wonders if he would have landed a spot on *The Oprah Winfrey Show* to dissect his decisions to reveal the most intimate and shameful details of his life, such as his sexual prowling, his abandonment of his children, and his frequent need to go to the bathroom. During his time fellow writer Dr. Samuel Johnson perhaps summed up the general reaction to the book best when he wrote to his friend James Boswell: "Rousseau, Sir, is a very bad man."

The modern memoir is an offshoot of traditional autobiography, but though the two forms share the same umbrella, they claim different ground. The memoir tends to reflect a life organized by theme—drug addiction, for example, or illness—while autobiography is typically a linear catchall, a succession of facts plodding from birth onward. Differences aside, narratives about the self, however they are structured, tend to have an itch to scratch, a bone to pick, so the author selects those damning details that stick in the reader's craw and make the story hard to shake. By confessing his own escapades and his conversion experience at the age of thirty-two, Augustine hoped to fulfill his grand ambition, to save Christianity from heretics and pagans and to "renew and exalt the faithful hearing of the gospel of man's utter need and God's abundant Grace," according to his biographer Albert Outler, in *Augustine: Confessions*. Likewise, the brilliant but paranoid Rousseau had already published several political tracts and novels that were immensely popular and that brought him into trouble with the authorities when, as a rebuttal to his critics, he penned a highly intimate memoir that exposed his search for integrity.

The power of the personal is evident in the lasting impressions both writers have made. Augustine's writings are perhaps second only to the Bible in their influence on Christian thought. Rousseau, in laying out the entrails of his life, inadvertently helped launch the emotionalism of the Romantic Movement, which eventually led to the French Revolution. Writers of memoir can, it is true, be guilty of self-absorption, but memoir can also be an important tool for forging connections among people, and thus individual stories, told well, have the power to change the world.

Scenes

Scenes, the primary building blocks of creative nonfiction, are little stories, episodes, anecdotes, or other opportunities for the creative nonfiction writer to be artful and use all the literary techniques available to fiction writers and dramatists. These techniques include dialogue, description, action, and suspense.

At their core, creative nonfiction stories are simply series of scenes, generally arranged according to some overall frame that makes them add up to a larger story.

Lauren Slater's "Three Spheres," for example, begins when Slater, a psychologist, is assigned a new patient, a very troubled woman with a history of self-mutilation and suicide attempts. Slater resists—clearly she does not want to care for this patient (we learn why later)—but her boss is insistent, and she has no choice but to relent.

Slater phones her new patient soon thereafter and immediately discovers in a brief conversation that the woman is severely traumatized. Slater calls 911 and quickly dispatches an ambulance so that paramedics can rescue the woman and take her to a nearby emergency room for treatment. Two days later Slater receives another phone call, from a nurse at the psychiatric hospital to which the patient has been admitted, summoning her to a team meeting to discuss the patient's treatment. Again Slater resists but eventually realizes that she must capitulate. Slater and the nurse agree on a time for the meeting and hang up.

Early in this essay, three episodes occur: three little stories or scenes in which something happens to further the action of the overall story. From beginning to end, in Slater's five-thousand-word essay, there are approximately a dozen scenes, all of which either advance the chronology of the story a little further or flash back to the past, offering insight and illumination. Why is Slater so resistant to caring for this patient? We find out through the scenes Slater provides, which chronicle the pain and tragedy of her own past.

How does a writer know that he or she is writing in scenes? Lee Gutkind has devised the yellow test, a simple exercise that helps writers recognize the definite narrative elements in their work. "Take a highlighter and yellow in the scenes," he says. "If half your essay, more or less, is not glaring and blaring back at you in yellow, that's a red flag, a warning that your essay may not be infused with enough narrative to compel a reader onward." The yellow test is a way of establishing that the writer is telling a story, showing rather than telling in as cinematic and intriguing a way as possible.

How to recognize a scene? "There is a difference between being scenic and descriptive and writing a real scene or story," says Gutkind. "It is not just pretty blue sky and scattered conversation, dialogue and description. A scene has a beginning and an end. Something has to happen."

What happens need not be monumental. Two people have a conversation and then say good-bye; a man walks down a street and sees something; a psychiatrist talks to her patient on the phone and then calls an ambulance. Each of these scenes can be used as a building block in a larger story.

Subjectivity

In traditional journalism, reporters are supposed to be objective, to maintain the style of an omniscient, invisible presence. This objectivity is an essential component of journalistic integrity. But writers like Tom Wolfe or Joan Didion, proponents of New Journalism, rejected this notion; instead they and other writers accepted as necessary the presence, personality, and perceptions of the author. New Journalism and its literary descendants acknowledged and even celebrated the writer's presence. The author/narrator interacts with other characters, comments upon events, and self-reflectively explores his or her personality in response to the developing story. Creative nonfiction is complexly structured by narrative voice, and the effectiveness of the piece depends, to a large extent, on the author's narrative presence.

For instance, in her classic essay "Slouching towards Bethlehem," Joan Didion examines 1967 San Francisco with a voice that is precise and emotionally detached. Instead of relying on her own reflections to convey meaning, she carefully chooses scenes and details that pack an emotional wallop. In the essay's last page and a half, she describes two young children ravaged by the drug scene. The only clue to her personal take on these children occurs in a single sentence: "I start to ask if any of the other children in High Kindergarten get stoned, but I falter at the key words."

Writers who, like Didion, choose to take a distanced stance can, to an extent, enhance the authority of their narrators. The writer's position as an outsider to the events of the story can potentially improve the story's credibility and grant greater freedom with respect to structure and point of view. Writers employing this strategy attempt to become camera lenses, points of perception that give enough details to allow the reader to come to his or her own conclusions.

Other writers inhabit their stories more fully. Ernest Hemingway's deeply personal perceptions of bullfighting pervade *Death in the Afternoon*, his revered 1932 tome on the sport. Hemingway implicates himself by admitting that he finds the goring of horses humorous. His confession allows him and the reader to get to the heart of the bullfighting ritual. "This is the sort of thing you should not admit," Hemingway writes. "[B]ut it is because such things have never been admitted that the bullfight has never been explained." Hemingway's willingness to explore his own reactions to the spectacle and to present himself as a sort of antihero helps give readers a more vivid and complete picture of the spectacle.

Writers who cast themselves as protagonists, as Hemingway does, allow their subjective experiences to compel their stories. As narrator/protagonist the writer can speak directly to the reader, comment on action and characters, interrupt the narrative flow with detailed descriptions or asides, and engage in philosophical reflection. On the other hand, first-person narrations are bound by the same limitations that we suffer in the world: It's more difficult to convey convincingly the thoughts and feelings of other characters.

The amount of subjectivity a writer grants him- or herself may be a matter of personal comfort, or it may depend upon the writer's relationship to the subject at hand. Unquestionably, however, the acknowledgment of writers' subjectivity adds depth to stories, and evidence of a writer's investment in a subject, far from distancing readers, can often add to a story's power to draw them in.

Tape Recording

The tape recorder would seem to be God's gift to writers, an invaluable tool for keeping accurate records of dialogues and interviews. Obviously, tape-recording affords the writer a certain amount of protection; a subject can't legitimately claim that he never said something if his words are committed to tape and can be played back as proof of the writer's accuracy. (Note that it's important, and in some cases required by law, to make sure subjects know they are being recorded.)

During the writing process, having tape recordings or transcripts at hand can be invaluable. And while cassette tapes can be somewhat unwieldy, annoying to rewind and fast-forward, prone to malfunctioning or exploding into ribbons of cellophane, such technological developments as digital recorders have made accessing recordings easier than ever by allowing writers to tab certain interesting spots of interviews, to download audio files directly into their computers, and even to make transcriptions using voice recognition software (instead of typing everything out or paying a transcription service or strapped-for-cash grad student).

Having access to tape recordings can "give texture" to a story, allowing writers to consider pauses, hesitations, tone, and other details that don't generally translate to a transcription or handwritten notes, says Ted Anthony, a veteran reporter and editor for the Associated Press and the author of *Chasing the Rising Sun*. "As writers we're given a tool kit that varies from generation to generation," Anthony says. "I've always thought the mark of a culture's competence is its ability to use the tools it has. If we're given digital recorders . . . why shouldn't we incorporate them into our work if they can give us things other tools can't?"

On the other hand, the process of procuring recordings may outweigh their benefits; some creative nonfiction writers believe that tape-recording actually hinders research.

"Taping makes me a lazy interviewer," says Alex Kotlowitz. "When you're taking notes, it forces you to concentrate on what you're hearing, to think of the next question," he told Robert S. Boynton in an interview.

Richard Preston, author of the true horror story of the possible outbreak of the Ebola virus, *The Hot Zone*, echoes Kotlowitz: "A tape recorder cannot capture a scene. A scene is kinesthetic." He claims it is simply unrealistic for him to tote a tape recorder everywhere he goes. He'd rather focus on the scene and the character and not worry over sentences that have to be arduously transcribed later. Recording can lull the writer into accepting a false, superficial sense of the truth and can intimidate subjects rather than relax them. Most important, according to Preston and other writers of his mind-set, a transcript does not tell a story (the interactions, the reactions, the facial expressions) while a narrative does.

Not that making do without a recording is easy. Writers who don't record generally take shorthand notes at a manic pace, run straight home, and type up their notes, adding details about scene and character that they noticed during the interview. But some writers, including Ted Conover, take no notes at all. "Taking notes alienates the very people I need to get close to," he says. (Conover's subjects are often hoboes, immigrants, and others who distrust reporters.) Instead he comes home and frequently writes "six to eight pages of exhaustive, single-spaced notes." He believes the presence of a tape recorder or a notepad would compromise the truth of the story he is trying to collect.

Other writers, including Jon Krakauer, champion using recordings. "Sure, there are situations where you can't record—like when you're in the backcountry for weeks and have to use batteries sparingly—but it is always better to tape if you can," Krakauer insists. "Do an interview in which you simultaneously use a tape recorder, and compare this to the handwritten record. I bet you'll find that you got many of the quotes wrong in your handwritten notes. Often you get the intent or the meaning right, but you miss the idiosyncratic phrasing, the precise inflections, the unique qualities that make a quote ring true. Quotes not based on a taped interview often sound more like the writer than the interview subject."

A subject's words tell only part of the story. The creative nonfiction writer asks: What is real? Does a recording rob reality of its color? How can you best discover the story beneath the story? Writers must ultimately find their own answers to these questions. Undoubtedly, the answer will depend, at least in part, on a writer's ability to recall what was said, on her style of interacting with subjects, and—perhaps most important—on what will work for each subject, in each story, carefully considered, case by case.

Truth

As philosophers have told us for centuries, passing the truth of immediate experience into some form that can be handed on to others is difficult. Troubled with levels and degrees, mixed with fact, memory, and interpretation, truth in storytelling is rarely black and white. We have come to accept that in fiction, truth emerges at a level higher than fact. Characters and events are imagined, but that doesn't mean the story isn't true on a higher or deeper level. Fiction explores the human heart and the emotional truth of human experience. As Picasso said, "Art is a lie that makes us realize the truth."

That may be, but creative nonfiction writing, though certainly an art, adheres to a slightly different standard. Consider Janet Cooke's experience. On September 29, 1980, she published an article in the *Washington Post* about the life of an eight-year-old heroin addict living on the street. "Jimmy's World" elicited a powerful emotional response from editors and readers. On April 13, 1981, Cooke was awarded a Pulitzer Prize. But she didn't keep it for very long.

The problem? The story was fabricated. Cooke tried to explain that her sources had hinted at the existence of a boy like Jimmy but that she had never met him. Writing the story, she decided to create a character that represented the experience of a child drug addict. The emotional truth of her story may have been real, but the facts of the story were false, and that made all the difference. Cooke was forced to resign her position at the newspaper and return the prize. For the nonfiction writer, manipulating facts and events in order to enhance narrative drive—that is, obfuscating or exaggerating literal or objective truth for dramatic effect—undermines the authority of the writer and destroys the trust of the reader. The writer cannot embellish, condense, or otherwise manipulate characters or events in order to make a more compelling story. If readers expect factual accuracy and they don't get it, they can easily feel betrayed and duped.

Readers of nonfiction (creative or otherwise) enter the text with an understanding that the story is linked directly not to the world of the possible but to the world of lived experience. It often reads like fiction and may involve the use of figurative language and literary techniques commonly found in fiction, and like fiction, it strives for the timeless emotional truths of human experience that bring us closer to a greater understanding of ourselves and each other. But creative nonfiction also explicitly engages the concept of the truth, both emotional and literal, and thus the writer of creative nonfiction is bound, by an implicit and sometimes explicit contract with the reader, to make sure the architecture of his story is based on authentic and reasonably verifiable experience.

Use of Imagination

Imagination, you may have been told, is the one place a non-fiction writer should never tread, but that advice is bad advice. The use of imagination is not what lands creative nonfiction writers in trouble; it is the *misuse* of imagination.

Certainly, we are—or should be—limited to only what is true when writing nonfiction, but what we imagine about something, someone, or some event is true in itself. It is true that we imagined it.

The important distinction here: truth in labeling.

For example, the writer of a childhood memoir should feel free to employ this (properly signaled) foray into invention: "I watched from the front window as my mother backed the family Chevy wildly out of the driveway, then sped up the empty street. I don't know where she was going, or why the rush, but at the time I felt sure she had a rendezvous with my father. I pictured them hugging just inside his new apartment, perhaps calling off the divorce, beginning our family reconciliation."

The author is a character in her own memoir, or should be, and it only enriches the story to know what she imagined as a child, where her fantasies took her. The passage makes clear where the author's observations end—the reckless driving—and where the speculation begins. The reader is no way misled.

Another example would be the use of speculation to fill a gap in a story that can't be closed by memory or research. "No one is certain," you might write, "what led Prendergast to return to Cleveland that summer, but it is possible that he was searching for the lost financial records, trying to restore his father's good name."

The imaginative brush can be used for small strokes, as in the examples just shown, or in far bolder ways. In her essay "Silent Dancing," for instance, Judith Ortiz Cofer intersperses short sections describing a home movie from her childhood with longer memories of the family's move from Puerto Rico to New Jersey. Eventually Cofer weaves in the narrative voice of a cousin who appears to her in a recurring dream, amplifying certain questions Cofer has about her own upbringing. By italicizing the cousin's dream comments, Cofer makes it clear that what she offers the reader comes partly from her imagination. It is accurate, nonetheless, a nonfiction account of the workings of her imagination.

Philip Gerard has taken the use of the nonfiction writer's imagination even a step further. In his essay "The Family Who Lived in the River," he recounts a story told to him by a friend, concerning a large Mexican immigrant family living in a makeshift cardboard-and-tin house along a dry riverbed west of Tucson. Gerard introduces the known facts: "A dozen or so people in all. They were a cheerful and energetic bunch. They spent the cool hours of morning and evening scavenging for discarded furniture and utensils or working to buy groceries." But eventually we reach a point where Gerard's friend loses touch with the family.

"When he returned," we are told, "he found out that there had been a big storm up in the mountains. When the water came rolling down the Santa Cruz, it carried away everything. The cardboard and tin house was gone."

Had Gerard limited himself to the known facts, that would have been the end of the brief essay. Instead it marks only the halfway point. After a section break, Gerard offers a possible ending, clearly signaling to the reader that he has created the scenario, one in which the family escapes the onrushing water. Then, after another section break, Gerard offers a second speculation, one in which the family's "lives are washed away."

The essay, it turns out, is not so much about the family, though what we learn about them is interesting, as about the unquenchable human urge to know what happened, to solve a mystery, to get to the bottom of some unknown circumstance. It is also an essay about storytelling and how the friend, the one who discovered the missing cardboard-and-tin house, needs to tell his version of the tale, even though it has no clear ending.

We all do this: fill in with our imaginations the parts of a story that intrigue us but that we can never really know. Nonfiction writers can do this as well, as long as they label it honestly.

The Vagaries of Memory

Human recollection is to a large extent a mystery. Combing through the shifting layers of time, we discover half ideas, fragmented scenes, and incomplete sentences. Details from significant life events are lost, while a kindergarten teacher's name is inscribed permanently in the mind. No one knows why our minds work as they do. As Lauren Slater notes in the Introduction to *Opening Skinner's Box*, "We are far from explaining why . . . we hold some memories and discard others, what those memories mean to us and how they shape a life." Often memories of key events, especially when traumatic, are the most elusive.

Take the case of Andre Dubus. In "Lights of the Long Night," he writes of a pedestrian/car accident in 1986 that left him permanently crippled and killed another man: "I remember the headlights, but I do not remember the car hitting Luis Santiago and me, and I do not remember the sounds our bodies made. . . . Then I was lying on the car's trunk and asking someone, 'What happened?'" Dubus laces his narrative of the accident with a list of what he can and cannot remember about that night. Ultimately he must rely on others' accounts to fill in the gaps of his own recollection. But many questions remain.

Readers share the writer's frustrating attempts to make meaning of that fatal night and conclude, with him, that "only Luis Santiago knows" what really happened. The accident has been erased from Dubus's own consciousness; he cannot re-create or revisit it in his mind, and the only person who might provide the answers has died. The truth has been lost.

Why is memory such a poor narrator, particularly at such crucial moments?

Slater explains that while science can demonstrate how certain responses get "encoded in the brain," the stuff of memory is unique and variable. "In the end," she says, "we are still the ones who weave, or not, still the ones who work the raw material into its final form and meaning."

Slater's authorial disclaimer raises questions for all memoirists: Do we remember only what we want to? Only what we must? And why do memories dangle, for years at a time, just beyond our reach?

In "Memory and Imagination," Patricia Hampl describes a scene from early childhood in which her father drops her off at her first piano lesson. Hampl provides the intricate details of the scene: Her piano teacher, Sister Olive, has to show her middle C twice. The room is full of sunlight and gleaming black pianos. Sister Olive has a sneezing spell, blames it on the excessive amount of sunlight in the room, and draws the shades.

"There must be a reason I remember that little story about my first piano lesson," Hampl reflects within her text. "No memoirist writes for long without experiencing an unsettling disbelief about the reliability of memory, a hunch that memory is not, after all, just memory."

But as she revisits the memory of her piano lesson, she realizes that not all aspects of the story are true. Her father might not have brought her to the lesson; her piano teacher may not have been named Olive. The truth is she doesn't remember her piano teacher at all. Hampl later says, "She's a sneeze in the sun and a finger touching middle C." The truth of the events lies waiting in the details. It is by culling through the particles of her memories that she determines what the meaning behind them is. "The beauty of memory rests in its talent for rendering detail, for paying homage to the senses, its capacity to love the particle of life. . . . If we learn not only to tell our stories but to listen to what our stories tell us—to write the first draft and then return for the second draft—we are doing the work for memory," Hampl notes.

Hampl concludes that her essay on the piano lesson has helped her identify the "touchstones" of the story of the piano lesson, which she believes is really an attempt to write about her father. Her job now is to sort through the details, to revisit them in her mind and to discern which ones really were a part of the piano lesson and why she is remembering them and what connection they have to her father. By engaging in this process, she attempts to illuminate why we recall what we recall. "What is remembered is what becomes reality," she writes. Thus the very act of writing conveys that despite the flaws and failure of memory, the price of forgetting is much higher—not just for the writer but for all of us.

Whose Story to Tell

In "Nonfiction in First Person, without Apology," Natalia Rachel Singer describes one of her first forays into nonfiction writing. Singer was sent by her journalism professor to follow the trail of the madam of a local brothel. In doing so, she encountered a subculture of complex and fascinating subjects.

At the end of her research Singer began to cull through her notes, digging for the story. "I was pressed with many writerly problems," she recounts. "How was I to deal with point of view? Whose story was it? The working women's? The clients'? My original goal had been to profile the madam, but she was swiftly being eclipsed by the prosecutor, the pediatrician, the necrophiliac and the priest, who were all far stranger than she was."

How do nonfiction writers determine whose story to tell when they approach a topic? There are, of course, factors that go into deciding whose experience and perspective to describe, especially when you write on assignment. Obviously, access to the subject and the subject's consent also must be taken into consideration. But a good rule of thumb is to write the story you would like to read. In other words, nonfiction writers usually tell the stories of people who entice them in one way or another.

For *Wonderland*, a profile of a modern American high school, Michael Bamberger spent a year immersed in the lives of the students of Pennsbury High School in Levittown, Pennsylvania. He focused primarily on a small cadre of students and the school's principal, threading their stories throughout the book. The mission of these related narratives, and that of the entire project, is to zoom in on the roles that these students play and overturn a few cultural assumptions by telling detailed stories of the individuals behind the labels. However, Bamberger's primary story is that of Bob Costa, an aspiring journalist and junior class president. Bob's is the voice we hear from the most frequently and the character whom we spend the most time following from scene to scene. Bamberger's choice to render the experiences and thoughts of this boy seems to be based largely on Bob's ambitious and charismatic persona, one that allows him to foray into the adult world of professional journalism despite his age. Perhaps because Bob fascinated Bamberger, Bamberger concluded that the boy would also fascinate his readers.

Bamberger is not alone in his method of selection. In an interview with David Hirschman in 2004, Gay Talese talked about his own decision-making process. Talese, who is celebrated for having written some of the twentieth century's most famous profiles, described the connections and instincts a writer must follow when choosing whose story to tell: "What draws me to people, in general, is that there is a vantage point that we share. There is something that I can hook into that is legitimately a part of these people's lives that I write about. It may not be full, but it is enough that I can go further with it." In other words, Talese is drawn to subjects in whom he sees a piece of himself.

On the other hand, writing can be a way to explore new worlds and ways of thinking. Susan Orlean, for example, has said she tells the stories of people she does not feel an immediate connection to. She chooses stories and experiences to write about based on a subject's passions—in *The Orchid Thief*, she writes, "I want to know what it feels like to care about something passionately"—and on the education the subject can give to her and consequently to the reader. She explained her philosophy further in an interview with Robert Boynton: "The only questions I pose of a topic are, 'Am I curious about this? Is there something here that I genuinely wonder about? Do I get excited and passionate about somebody else's passion?'"

Like Orlean, who built a best seller around an obsessive poacher of plants, good nonfiction writers find and portray complex protagonists who have universal appeal. But even charisma is no guarantee that a character is the best center for a story. As many new writers, including the young Natalia Singer, have discovered, there is no single formula for whose story to tell. Sometimes your story picks you rather than the other way around. The role each subject will play in your work never consistently reveals itself at any one time in the researching or writing process. Some speak to you from the start; others lie in hiding, waiting to be discovered.

Writers' Responsibility to Subjects

In *The Journalist and the Murderer*, Janet Malcolm focuses on a libel suit between Jeffrey MacDonald, a convicted murderer, and the celebrity biographer he hired to write his story, as a way of examining the relationship between writer and subject. While writing this book, Malcolm was sued by one of her own subjects, Jeffrey Masson, who contended that Malcolm misquoted him in order to defame him. Perhaps Malcolm's experience with Masson infused her writing with an extra dose of bitterness. In any event, in *The Journalist and the Murderer* she sharply delineates the stakes for writer and subject: "Every journalist who is not too stupid or full of himself to notice what is going on knows that what he does is morally indefensible. He is a kind of confidence man, preying on people's vanity, ignorance or loneliness, gaining their trust and betraying them without remorse."

But Malcolm also notes that in general, subjects have just as many selfish motives and biases as writers: "Of course, at the bottom, no subject is naïve. . . . [E]very subject of writing knows on some level what is in store for him and remains in the relationship anyway, impelled by something stronger than his reason."

Journalists, Malcolm reminds us, never have any intention

of writing their subjects' autobiographies for them. The subjects, however, frequently do not know this until their stories appear in print, at which point they are often disappointed or resentful:

> The catastrophe suffered by the subject is no simple matter of an unflattering likeness or misrepresentation of his view; what pains him, what rankles and sometimes drives him to extremes of vengefulness, is the deception that has been practiced on him.

Lauren Slater encountered similar trouble when writing about Harvard psychologist Jerome Kagan in *Opening Skinner's Box*, her book about the controversial work of the late Harvard psychologist B. F. Skinner. (Skinner was a champion of behaviorism, a school of psychology that attributes behavior to positive reinforcement—think Pavlov's dog—and denies the existence of free will.) Kagan, a contemporary and colleague of Skinner's and renowned in his own right as an expert on early childhood development, knew the behaviorist for years, so he was a natural choice for Slater to interview. When she asked Kagan if he believed that free will did in fact exist, he ducked under his desk. "I'm under my desk," he shouted up to her. "I've never gotten under my desk before. Is this not an act of free will?"

When the book was published, Kagan, along with other subjects Slater had interviewed (including Skinner's daughter Deborah), claimed that she had misrepresented him. Specifically, he denied that he had ever gotten under his desk. (When the *New York Times* subsequently questioned Slater about his allegations, she was able to produce an e-mail in which Kagan seemed to acknowledge his unusual behavior.)

Who is in the wrong here? That question is not easily answered. Ultimately, Kagan was as motivated to defend his professional views on psychology, not to mention the dignity of his public persona, as Slater was to get her story. Ultimately, the communication between subject and writer is always a double-edged sword. While writers have considerable editorial power, their subjects invariably have impressive agendas of their own and the ability to derail communication or refuse to share information. The final responsibility, however, is the writer's; he or she is the one to reproduce the information provided by the subject for an audience. We can't know for certain what occurred or what was said in Slater's interview with Kagan; instead we are reliant on Slater's account of the events.

The question then is what impels the writer. Malcolm maintains that journalists justify their dominance by invoking the phrases "freedom of speech" and "the public's right to know," their commitment to journalism as an art form, and, more simply, their own need to survive professionally. Another common, morally defensible answer is that one person's truth is better than no truth at all. Nonetheless, writers have an ethical responsibility to consider the ways in which their stories may continue to affect their subjects' lives, even long after publication.

About the Contributors

Robert S. Boynton is the director of NYU's Magazine Writing Program. He is the author of *The New New Journalism* (Vintage Books, 2005) and has been an editor at *Manhattan, Inc.* and *Harper's*. He has written for the *New Yorker*, the *New York Times Magazine*, the *Atlantic Monthly*, the *Nation, Lingua Franca, Bookforum*, the *New York Times Book Review*, the *Los Angeles Times Book Review*, the *Village Voice, Rolling Stone*, and many other publications.

Kristen Cosby's work has appeared in *Fourth Genre*, and her essays have garnered Finalist for the 2005 *Iowa Review* Prize and Honorable Mention for *Fourth Genre*'s Editor's Prize.

Taha Ebrahimi has written for the *Seattle Times*, and her nonfiction writing has earned awards from the Pacific Northwest Writers Association, the *Bellingham Review*, Hedgebrook Writers Colony, and the Thomas J. Watson Foundation. A Seattle native, she currently teaches composition while pursuing an M.F.A. in creative nonfiction at the University of Pittsburgh.

Hattie Fletcher is the managing editor of *Creative Nonfiction* and a coordinating editor for the Best Creative Nonfiction series.

Lee Gutkind's most recent book, *Almost Human: Making Robots Think*, details his experiences at the Robotics Institute at Carnegie Mellon University. Gutkind's immersion into the motorcycle subculture (*Bike Fever*), the organ transplant milieu (*Many Sleepless Nights*), and other previously unmined worlds has led to nine books and many award-winning literary achievements. Gutkind is also the editor of several anthologies, including the Best Creative Nonfiction series. He is a professor of English at the University of Pittsburgh and the founder and editor of *Creative Nonfiction*.

Meredith Hall is the 2004 recipient of the Gift of Freedom Award, a two-year writing grant from A Room of Her Own Foundation. She also received the Maine Arts Commission's Individual Artist Fellowship. She won the 2005 *Pushcart Prize* and was named in "Notable Essays" in *The Best American Essays 2005*. Her work has appeared in the *New York Times*, the *Southern Review*, *Creative Nonfiction*, *Five Points*, and many other journals and anthologies. Her memoir, *Without a Map*, was recently published by Beacon Press. She teaches writing at the University of New Hampshire and lives on the coast of Maine.

Donna Hogarty is a creative nonfiction M.F.A. candidate at the University of Pittsburgh. She has written for *Reader's Digest*, *Ladies' Home Journal*, *Woman's Day*, and other magazines.

Kristen Iversen is the author of the best-selling biography *Molly Brown: Unraveling the Myth* (winner of the Colorado

Book Award for biography) and the textbook *Shadow Boxing: Art and Craft in Creative Nonfiction*. A forthcoming memoir, *Full Body Burden*, chronicles her experiences with Rocky Flats, a government facility near Denver that secretly produced plutonium triggers for nuclear bombs. She currently teaches at the University of Memphis and is the editor in chief of the *Pinch*.

Lori Jakiela is the author of a memoir, *Miss New York Has Everything*. Her chapbook, *The Regulars*, was published by Liquid Paper Press. Her work has appeared in literary magazines and anthologies, including *DoubleTake*, *Chicago Review*, *5 AM*, *River Styx*, and *Brevity*. She lives in Pittsburgh.

Barbara Lounsberry's books include *The Art of Fact: Contemporary Artists of Nonfiction* (1992), *The Writer in You* (1994), *Writing Creative Nonfiction: The Literature of Reality* (coedited with Gay Talese, 1996), and *The Tales We Tell: Perspectives on the Short Story* (1998; coedited with Susan Lohafer). She is currently completing a book about Virginia Woolf's diaries and the diaries Woolf read.

Brenda Miller is the author of *Season of the Body*, a finalist for the PEN American Center Book Award in Creative Nonfiction. She has received four Pushcart Prizes, and her essays have appeared in periodicals including the *Sun*, *Creative Nonfiction*, *Fourth Genre*, *Utne Reader*, and the *Georgia Review*. She coauthored, with Suzanne Paola, the textbook *Tell It Slant: Writing and Shaping Creative Nonfiction*. She is an associate professor of English at Western Washington University and the editor in chief of the *Bellingham Review*.

Dinty W. Moore is the author of the memoir *Between Panic and Desire*, forthcoming from the University of Nebraska Press, and the editor of *Brevity*, the online journal of extremely brief nonfiction. He teaches at Ohio University.

Paul Morris teaches creative nonfiction writing at Arizona State University, where he directs the Master of Liberal Studies program. His poems, translations, and essays have appeared in such journals as *the threepenny review*, *Crazyhorse*, *Translation*, *Black Warrior Review*, *Hayden's Ferry Review*, and *Alaska Quarterly*, and he has been nominated for three Pushcart Awards.

Dennis Palumbo is a writer and licensed psychotherapist in private practice, specializing in creative issues. His latest book, *Writing from the Inside Out*, is published by John Wiley and Sons. His screenwriting credits include the feature film *My Favorite Year*, and he was a staff writer for the television series *Welcome Back, Kotter*. He is currently a contributing writer to the *New York Times* and the *Lancet* and does commentary for NPR's *All Things Considered*.

Lori Pfeiffer's work has appeared in *Arizona Highways*, *Working Woman*, *America West Airlines Magazine*, *Black Enterprise*, and the anthology *Mamaphonic: Balancing Motherhood and Other Creative Acts*. She has taught creative nonfiction at Arizona State University and Phoenix College. She is currently at work on *The Mother's Muse: Notes on Writing and Raising Children*.

Mimi Schwartz's latest book is *Good Neighbors, Bad Times: Echoes of My Father's German Village* (University of Nebraska

Press). Other books are *Thoughts from a Queen-Sized Bed,* *Writing for Many Roles,* and *Writing True: The Art and Craft of Creative Nonfiction* (with Sondra Perl). Her short work has appeared in the *Missouri Review, Creative Nonfiction, Fourth Genre, Tikkun,* the *New York Times,* and the *Writer's Chronicle,* among others. Five of her essays have been Notables in *Best American Essays.*

Bryant Simon is a professor of history and director of American studies at Temple University. He is finishing a book about Starbucks, forthcoming from Bloomsbury Press.

Kathleen Tarr teaches writing at the University of Alaska, Anchorage. She received her M.F.A. in creative nonfiction writing from the University of Pittsburgh.

Sarah Z. Wexler holds a B.A. and an M.F.A. in writing from the University of Pittsburgh, where she won the 2006 Creative Nonfiction Award. She currently lives in New York, where she works for *Marie Claire.* Her writing has appeared in *Esquire, Wired, Popular Science, Esquire's Big Black Book, Ladies' Home Journal,* and the *Washington Post.*

Susan Yohe is a shareholder with Buchanan Ingersoll & Rooney PC, practicing in the Commercial Litigation Group. She has handled a range of litigation matters, including intellectual property, antitrust, First Amendment, and professional malpractice cases.

Acknowledgments

This has been an ensemble effort; the strength of this book is the combined voices and wisdom of the writers and editors who have together shaped *Keep It Real*. We thank them, as well as our editor at Norton, Amy Cherry, and our always supportive agent, Andrew Blauner.

We also thank the Pennsylvania Council on the Arts and the Juliet Lea Hillman Simonds Foundation, both of which provide ongoing support for the Creative Nonfiction Foundation's projects.

Finally, we would like to thank the National Endowment for the Arts for its support of the issue of *Creative Nonfiction* that has now become this book.